The Lucky One

DALE ARENSON

Paperback ISBN: 979-8-9876398-9-4
Hardcover ISBN: 979-8-9876398-8-7

YOU can break away or YOU can stay,
YOU choose YOUR life, YOU'Re free to fly
Go on and fly
Go on and fly

~ Laura Branigan, The Lucky One

Contents

Introduction

Having mostly left behind my wild life as an outlaw biker, then having my subsequent adventures in the wilds of Alaska, I was on the path to reinventing myself as a pilot.

At the end of book one, I had parted ways with world-famous airshow pilot Bob Hoover and his announcer, Jim Driskell. This, in itself, had been the opportunity of a lifetime.

The ten days I was with them had flown by. It interrupted my do-it-yourself flight training, but I gained an enormous amount of confidence from being around all the famous people I met and from watching Bob do almost impossible things with airplanes.

I came back with a renewed commitment to a future in aviation. More focused than ever, I was almost obsessed with flying. I doubled down on my studying during the day and on my flight training at night. I was careful to balance my time, whether I was back with the motorcycle club or pursuing my new passion.

But it wasn't all blue skies and tailwinds.

No fate but what we make.

~Sarah Conner

Prologue

Headhunter

Despair seemed to fill my being as I sat on the edge of my bed in a dark studio apartment in Van Nuys, California. My dead-end life had caught up with me, and the dark specter of suicide kept popping into my mind as a solution.

When I closed my eyes, the fog inside my head became one of those cartoons. On one shoulder stood an angel saying, "No, don't do it. You have so much to live for." Meanwhile, a little devil stood on my left shoulder (isn't it always the left shoulder?), saying, "Go ahead, do it! What are you waiting for? It will solve all your problems. Don't wait. Do it now."

The angel on the right shoulder kept saying, "Nooo, nooo!"

I felt like a complete failure, like I was going nowhere. I hated my job and was living a life I didn't want. Alone, away from family and friends. How had I gotten here?

My employer was paying for the tiny apartment. It was the only compensation I'd received. My job paid only commission, and I had not made a dime since starting this nightmare a month prior.

Now the month was up. Would my boss pay for another month's rent given that I had not produced a single account? It seemed like zero hour... decision time.

It was a good thing I was too broke to buy alcohol. Food was hard enough to get.

I was a "headhunter." No, not a hitman, though for me that might have been easier! Officially known by the nice name of "executive recruiter," I sat in a cubicle all day cold-calling businesses, talking to people I didn't know about things I didn't understand, trying to hook people up with jobs for other businesses or finding a certain applicant for an open slot.

After failing at selling air freight, I'd convinced my new boss I could do the job. I needed work and was willing to try anything, as I was desperate to avoid going back to construction. Somehow, it seemed that would be going backward, and I wanted to move forward.

But I wasn't good at this job and now all I wanted was out. I felt I owed my boss for giving me a chance and paying for this apartment, but I was so unhappy, I just wanted this to end.

Sleep seemed impossible and the prospect of getting up in the morning and going back to that cubicle was too much to bear.

How do you sleep when your worst nightmare is waking up and going to work?

This was June 1979. Just a few months earlier, I had flown my Cessna 140 from Alaska to Southern California to start a new life. However, my plan for that new life included a career in aviation, and right now that seemed a world away.

A commercial pilot license would cost a lot of money, and I could barely afford to eat and put gas in my car.

My goals seemed far away and out of reach. It felt like I was being unrealistic, and I would never get there.

My mood was as dark as the small room. I was exhausted but unable to sleep. The dimly lit clock radio said it was just past 2 AM. I needed to move forward, but I felt like I was stuck in quicksand. I needed to rest and sleep but couldn't do either.

It didn't help that I had no one to talk it over with. A year before, in Alaska, my wife had moved out to live with someone who I'd thought was a friend. So, I'd continued my life alone, wanting only to pursue my dream of flying. Yes, I was now a pilot, but I was so broke that I couldn't afford to put gas in my cheap little two-seat airplane. My plan to work as a pilot seemed to have come to a screeching halt. I could sell the airplane, but the bank owned it anyway. Plus, what would I use to get my ratings to become a commercial pilot?

I wanted to be responsible and do the job I had promised I would do, but I hated it. Every half hour, it seemed, the boss poked his head in and asked why I wasn't on the phone. Why hadn't I gotten any results? When I saw the frustrated, angry look on his face, I wasn't sure who I disliked more: him or me.

Now, late at night, my mind searched for solutions. I seemed to be at an impasse and cursed myself for the suicidal thoughts, but they kept coming back.

A permanent solution to a temporary problem.

I never got far enough to think about exactly how I would do it. Turn on the oven without lighting it? It was an electric stove. Fortunately, I had no gun with me.

Pacing the small, dark apartment, I finally concluded that something had to be done, now! And it wouldn't be *that*!

The biggest thing stopping me wasn't the act itself, but what it would do to the few people I knew and the fewer people who loved me. That thought was unbearable. I was inflicting enough pain on myself, and I didn't want to hurt anyone else.

With that in mind, and sleep being out of the question, I made my decision. Turning on the lights, I pulled on my jeans, a black T-shirt, and a Levi's jacket, then started throwing my few belongings into a gunny sack. Leaving the half-quart of milk and two eggs in the fridge, I used the phone on the wall to dial the office. When the answering machine picked up, I said, "This is Dale. I won't be in today, or ever. I'm sorry, I'm not cut out for this job. Thank you for giving me a chance."

I left the key on the counter and closed the unlocked door behind me. Walking to my car parked on Haskell Avenue, I threw my bag in the back seat and turned the key on the 1974 Ford Mustang Two, which was nothing more than a Ford Pinto with a fancier body style. Despite being only five years old, it already seemed like a junker.

After a few short blocks, I got onto the southbound entrance to the 405 freeway. At Sherman Oaks, I turned east on the 101. Traffic was a breeze at that time of night. Two hours later, the eastern sky was starting to turn pale orange, then blue as I arrived at my retired mother's rented single-wide mobile home outside Hemet, California.

After letting myself in with a key from under a potted plant, I tip-toed across the creaking floor to the empty spare bedroom that was just big enough for a single twin bed. Kicking off my boots, but still dressed, I lay in the dark and stared up at the ceiling. My mind began to clear. I felt like a huge weight had been lifted from my shoulders, and I could breathe again.

I had decided to do whatever it took to work toward my flying career and not waste time at any job that interfered with my goal. After all the brushes with death I'd had in my convoluted life, this time, for once, I felt that I'd saved my own life.

No man is luckier than he who thinks himself so.

~Proverb

Chapter 1
One year later

The noise was deafening as I rode in a pack of over two hundred motorcycles, mostly chopped Harleys ridden by greasy, long-haired bikers. Many of them were my friends and club brothers.

With the wind in my face and only a pair of sunglasses for protection, the roaring of the wind in my ears was matched by the machine gun-like exhaust of the iron horses ridden by twentieth-century outlaws.

It was another perfect California day with bright sunshine breaking through the usual smog and warm enough to not need a jacket.

We sped along in formation on the freeway in east Los Angeles, riding fast, close, and dangerous. Fortunately, this time there was no wild police chase.

The pack was two abreast and a mile long. I stomped on the "suicide" foot clutch and shifted gears with my left hand, jockeying to stay in position and keep the spacing tight with the bike in front of me.

Shiny machines – most with long front ends – flashed chrome and bright paint jobs. The riders wore leather and Levi's with heavy boots – hard and tough, with attitudes to match. I still felt at home in this crowd.

We were "One Percenter" motorcycle clubs, mostly Hangmen and Hessians, but others too.

This wasn't the 1960s or 70s. It was 1980. The irony of this moment wasn't lost on me. Just one month before, I'd been traveling with aviation legend Bob Hoover on part of his airshow circuit.

Now I was back in my old environment of bikes and bikers – a lifestyle I popped in and out of as needed.

The reason for this big pack was a funeral for the president of the Orange County chapter of the Hessians. His name was Dennis Decker, or "Dirty Dennis." He'd been a friend of mine.

Ten years prior he had prospected for the Hangmen. At the time, I was just a hang-around. Dennis never made it in and I never asked him why. Instead, he'd joined the Hessians. Now, a decade later, he'd risen to president of the OC chapter.

Two weeks ago, they'd been on a run in the desert. We used to do that all the time, to get away in some remote location with no citizens around. ("Citizens" meant normal people). We'd camp out, drink, take drugs, and shoot guns for target practice – not a good combination.

They were supposed to be having fun as the party continued into the night. Then it went badly.

The wind was blowing, and the building clouds could be seen as lightning flashed and crawled across the sky like an electric spiderweb. Thunder rumbled across the desert. It was a dark and stormy night, as Snoopy would say. But the weather wasn't the only ominous thing in the air.

One member had a little too much drugs and alcohol. Perhaps whisky and probably something psychedelic. For some reason, he was in a bad mood.

Standing on the porch of an old, abandoned building in the ghost town where they'd camped, the Hessian started waving a gun around while yelling, swearing, and making threats. That wasn't acceptable, even in this crowd.

Despite the obvious danger, Dennis – being the president – left the side of the bonfire, walked up steps of the old wooden porch, and confronted the guy. I don't remember his name and don't care to.

Dennis looked him in the eye, held out his hand, and said, "Give me the gun."

The drugged-up member's response was to shoot Dennis in the face, killing him instantly.

Seeing their president cut down, several other Hessians, without hesitation, pulled out their guns, thoroughly and fatally ventilating the drugged-up murderer.

And then the storm hit.

It was a bad night all around. But then, that was the life of outlaw bikers.

In my previous life, I'd been in similar situations. Thankfully, I wasn't there that night.

Now the pack slowed to exit the freeway, taking an off-ramp into the cemetery. It felt surreal as I geared down, following the line of Harleys and grim-faced bikers.

I was trying to make my way into a new life in the world of aviation, but here I was on a bike in my old riding clothes, wearing my cut again, like a time warp. Returning to the past. My past, to stroll through the landscape of violence, drugs, and death.

In the cemetery, still in formation, we swung into the roadway and lined up, side by side, before backing our bikes to the curb at the location for the gravesite. It felt so familiar and, yet, so foreign.

The deafening rumble subsided into an eerie silence as the big V-twin engines were shut off and we threw out our kickstands. There was little talking and no laughter.

Standing on a grassy hillside overlooking a smoggy valley, I was shoulder to shoulder with all the bikers crowding around the gravesite at Forest Lawn Cemetery in Los Angeles. I watched the two Hessians being buried together, side by side. My friend and his killer.

It was a world that I'd been part of, but it now seemed to be another world.

When the ceremony was over, I was happy to ride away.

I was riding away not just from the funeral but from my past, hopefully into a new world, a new life in the sky that I hoped would be my future.

Forest Lawn Cemetery, 1980

There is no elevator to success, you have to take the stairs.

~Unknown

Chapter 2

A classroom in the sky

Curt said, "You need to get a flight instructor's rating."

I said, "I don't want to be a flight instructor. I want a real flying job."

"You want to be as good a pilot as possible, don't you?"

"Of course."

"Well, the best way to learn about anything is to teach it to others. You need to get your CFI."

"Okay." I sighed, knowing Curt was right. He had been not only my close friend but also a club brother for years and was both a licensed flight instructor and an instrument instructor. He had already helped me enormously in my quest to become a professional pilot. If he told me I needed something, then I needed it.

After moving back to Hemet from Van Nuys, I answered a want ad in the local paper. The Skyline motorhome factory needed a salesperson. The sales manager was a private pilot, and when he found out I was too, he hired me. There was a small salary plus commission. However, because of the high gas prices, motorhomes were not selling, so they put me in charge of warranty work. No commission but the monthly pay was higher.

I was there for about six months. The money helped me get my commercial and multi-engine rating. As soon as my boss found that out, he laid me off, saying, "You're just going to get a flying job now anyway. You won't need this anymore."

The truth was, they wanted to get rid of me because I was too generous with the customers, approving almost any repairs that came in the door. It was costing them too much money.

I applied for unemployment insurance and started working on my instrument rating.

Pilot jobs were few and far between, and the 1980s "malaise" economy was still in recession and getting worse. The high unemployment numbers wouldn't get better for another two years.

It wasn't a good time to look for a job, let alone start a new career.

Before my adventures with Bob Hoover, I had qualified as a commercial multi-engine pilot and instrument pilot, but I still had a long way to go. I hadn't been able to find a flying job.

My little Cessna 140 didn't have the instrumentation and radios for me to obtain the necessary training. So, I continued to rent newer aircraft like a Beechcraft C24R Sierra from Riverside Air Service in Riverside, California.

It was the same model I had flown the year before with Jay Johnson in McCook, Nebraska. A modern "complex" airplane, it had retractable landing gear, a constant speed propeller, and all the necessary advanced radios.

I'd been studying to take my flight instructor's written test, as Curt had advised. It was tedious book work! The flying part was always more fun.

For a pilot, it is always a thrill to fly higher-performance airplanes. Every faster airplane is a step up from what you know.

Tom and I with his Bonanza

In my spare time, Curt, Uncle Tom, Joe Heller, and I flew everywhere. Avgas was slightly more costly than car gas, but not much, and we had our own planes. Airshows were a favorite destination, sometimes at Chino, Mojave, or even up to Reno, Nevada at the annual air races. We'd see my friends Bob Hoover and Jim Driskell and help them with their shows.

Introducing Curt to Bob Hoover.

At the Mojave Air Races one year, I met Greg "Pappy" Boyington, the legend from Baa Baa Black Sheep. He was an American hero, World War II fighter pilot, and Medal of Honor recipient. I'd read his book, and just a few years prior, actor Robert Conrad had played him in the television series.

He autographed his book for me, and we chatted about flying while Uncle Tom snapped a couple of pictures of us. He seemed to be a genuine down-to-earth guy. I was honored to make his acquaintance.

With WW2 Ace Pappy Boyington at the Mojave Air Races

In the booth next to him was the highest-scoring Japanese ace Saburo Sakai, selling and signing his book "Samurai." Former enemies, he and Boyington had become good friends.

Another legendary airshow performer and a close friend of Bob Hoover was Art Scholl. Flying his "Super Chipmunk," he was an airshow favorite, usually with his dog Aileron in the cockpit with him.

When not doing airshows and photography for Hollywood movies like *The Great Waldo Pepper* and the TV show "CHiPs," Art ran an FBO at Rialto Airport. We used to stop in there from time to time, and Art was frequently there – just a normal, everyday guy, running his business, whom you could talk about flying with. Like Hoover, he was an incredibly qualified pilot with a Ph.D. and had been a professor and the head of the Department of Aeronautics at San Bernardino Valley College. He quit to go into airshow performing full time.

I saw a statistic that said, in 1968, the planet had just under four billion people on it – about half of what it is now. Looking back, it seems like it was easier to meet famous people and that they were less shielded from the public.

In 1985 Art Scholl was doing some filming for the movie *Top Gun* off the coast of California near Carlsbad. He was trying to get footage of a flat spin. His Pitts S-2 biplane wouldn't come out of the spin, and he crashed into the ocean. He and the airplane were never found. The movie is dedicated to him.

Art Scholl in the Super Chipmunk with his dog, Aileron.

Life was fun and interesting, but as far as my flying career was concerned, I felt like I was going nowhere while I studied and trained. Then, suddenly, time was fast-forwarded like a VHS tape.

I'd had a commercial/multi-engine rating for ten months. In May I passed my instrument rating, and on October 4, 1980 I completed my check ride for Certificated Flight Instructor, or CFI.

I'd done it all on a shoestring with Curt's help while studying for the written tests on my own.

There was a new FBO in Hemet. It was a startup operation with the intent of being a flight school and Piper Aircraft dealership. When they found out I was now an instructor, the owner immediately offered me a job. I was amazed. I didn't even have to leave town for my first flying job.

I was finally a working commercial pilot, not only as a flight instructor but as a charter pilot as well! I'd be flying high-performance airplanes taking people to or from locations like Los Angeles International, Las Vegas, and many other destinations.

Initially, I was the only pilot. They had a fleet of leased aircraft that I'd have to get checked out in: a Piper Turbo Arrow, a six-seat Piper Lance, and a twin-engine Piper Seneca. They were all high-performance airplanes with retractable landing gear. Plus, there was a little two-seat trainer called the PA-38 Tomahawk, which had been out only since 1978.

The Piper Tomahawk.

There was no one to train me and check me out in the planes, but I'd already flown a lot of different aircraft. After being around Bob Hoover and watching him do incredible maneuvers over and over in different kinds of airplanes, I'd gained a lot of confidence. All airplanes are different, but they are the same in most ways. I felt if I could fly one, I could fly them all.

So, I read the aircraft manuals, one at a time, studied the systems, memorized the V-speeds required, and took them out and flew them.

It might not have been legal, but I didn't ask, and the owner didn't say anything. Just like that, I was "qualified" in those four airplanes. I'd checked myself out.

I was now on my way, having achieved my dream of being a working pilot. I almost starved to death because of how little money I made. It's amazing how many ways you can cook Top Ramen noodles. But I didn't care. I was where I wanted to be. I felt successful and I was happy.

Just over two years had passed since I'd gotten my private pilot license. Five and a half years earlier I'd taken a break from the motorcycle club and moved to Alaska to get a job on the pipeline.

There are faster ways to do what I did. If you could afford to go to an aviation university, or if your father was a flight instructor and owned an airplane, you might do it cheaper. But I think it would be impossible to have done it faster and on less money.

Success is not the key to happiness. Happiness is the key to success. If you love what you are doing, you will be successful.

~ Herman Cain

Chapter 3
Getting paid to fly

Much to my surprise, not only did I enjoy flight instructing but I was good at it. I started building a clientele of students. My pay was ten dollars per flight hour but nothing on the preflight briefings on the ground. Some days I'd make twenty to thirty dollars, while other days I'd make nothing. Most of my students learned easily and said they liked my instructing style. I told them I had to do that for my sake: Keep it simple, stupid.

Charter flights with passengers or ferrying airplanes from one place to another also paid ten dollars per flight hour. I was happy to get whatever flight time I could, and it was such a pleasure to go places other than the practice area or stay in the airport traffic pattern.

I was building up time and experience and getting paid for it. Who could ask for more? It was a turning point in my career.

Eventually the little flight school brought in enough students that my buddy Curt could help with the extra duties. Many of my students became friends.

I struck up a friendship with a married couple who were both flight students. Their names were Tom and Jeri — easy to remember, like the cat and mouse cartoon. Tom was a businessman, and his lovely wife Jeri was a nurse. They both wanted to learn to fly, although Jeri said, "I'm afraid to fly, but the way he drives, I'm not getting into an airplane with him unless I know how to fly it too."

Unlike me, they were accomplished people. As I got to know them, they invited me to what they called a mastermind class that they attended a couple of times a week. It was only about eight or ten people, who included a lawyer, a real estate agent, and a CPA.

They'd talk about goals in their jobs or businesses and how to achieve them, and everyone would support each other's aspirations and desires. Something about verbalizing your intentions had a way of bringing them to life.

Once, a conversation went around the room in which attendees were asked, "What are your financial goals?"

I was surprised that most of them said they wanted to be millionaires and that they even had plans on how to make that happen.

To me, that sounded bizarre. A millionaire. How absurd. Why not just ask for the stars?

Putting me on the spot, Tom looked at me and said, "So, how much money do you want to make?"

Having just started out as a flight instructor, and given the way things were going, I figured I'd be lucky to make three thousand dollars a year.

I said, "I don't know. I hadn't thought about it."

"You must have an idea. What do you need to live on?"

"When I was married in Alaska, my wife made a thousand dollars a month before taxes. I envied her making that much."

The CPA, a lady named Ann, said, "That's not enough. Don't think about what you need. Think about what you want."

"I want to be a successful pilot. The money is secondary."

Tom said, "Who do you know who makes a lot of money?"

"I have an old friend who works really hard driving a long-haul truck. He told me he makes thirty thousand a year. That seems like a lot of money."

Someone said, "It's not that much. You should aim higher."

"I don't want to be unrealistic. I'll stick with thirty thousand as my goal."

Tom said, "What about the airlines? I'm sure they make good money."

These people didn't know me very well, and I wasn't about to tell them my background: high school dropout and an arrest record from when I was a biker. They thought I was a normal person. I said, "There's no way. They require college, and I don't have any."

Someone said, "Go to college then."

I looked at the floor and shook my head, knowing it wouldn't erase the arrest record.

But I appreciated their efforts and concern. Once again, I was around positive people. They were practically strangers, but they cared about my future. It has a way of energizing you. I read somewhere, "You can't hang out with negative people and have a positive life." I'd already experienced a lot of negative and I had no desire to go back.

I'd already proven to myself the power of imagination: an outlaw biker and construction worker transforming himself into an auto parts salesman and then a pilot. I knew I was on the right track.

Like in Alaska, these new friends got me to read more books on positive thinking. I knew where I wanted to go and how to get there. I just needed more experience and qualifications.

Fortunately, I loved flying airplanes and was practically obsessed with it. All the hard work didn't seem like work. An old quote equally attributed to Confucius and Mark Twain says, "Find a job you love, and you will never have to work a day in your life."

In between the charter flights, where I felt like a "real" pilot, I was instructing students. Sometimes they'd try to kill me. Not intentionally, of course, but it made life interesting.

You had to be on your toes and ready to take over the controls, especially on landing. It required split-second timing. With new students, if you took over too soon, they didn't learn for themselves. If you waited too long, you might crash. And guess who was at fault... if you survived.

Curt was right when he said, "If you really want to learn about something, you have to teach it."

I learned more about flying by being a flight instructor than I could have imagined. To my surprise, I loved it. Best of all, I was getting paid for it.

The world of motorcycles, as fun as it was, was only two-dimensional. Airplanes added the vertical, and now life was three-dimensional. But then there was the dimension of radio contact. Was that the fourth dimension? The disembodied voice? The world of air traffic control was also fascinating.

I was now flying all kinds of airplanes and imparting knowledge and skills to new pilots. At the time, I took it for granted. I wanted to move up, fly bigger and faster airplanes, and make more money. But looking back, I realize it was a magical period. I was still a relatively new pilot nurturing even newer pilots into the world of aviation. I flew every moment I could.

One of the reasons Piper developed the Tomahawk was so it would spin better than the Cessna 150 and 152, which are so stable they would fly themselves out of a spin. The Tomahawk needed more positive input to get it out.

It required more skill on the pilot's part, even though the FAA had not required spin training for private pilots since 1949. It was still required for flight instructors.

I liked to teach spins and spin recovery to my students anyway, once they were up to it. It was a great confidence builder.

One student refused to properly use the rudders. When I badgered him, he'd say, "Why do I have to?"

Just explaining it to him didn't seem to be good enough. So, while at a safe altitude, I showed him the old "overshooting final approach at low altitude cross-controlled stall" routine.

The little Tomahawk obediently snapped into a spin, and the whole world whirled round and round as we plunged what seemed to be straight down. The airframe was rumbling, and that T-tail was shaking like it wanted to tear itself off.

After three turns, I recovered, but it scared him so badly that this was his last lesson. It was just as well; no instructor wants to produce a student who will be dangerous.

Eventually the FAA put out a directive forbidding the Tomahawk to be spun. It turned out that the accident rate for spins in the little T-bird was three to five times higher than that for the Cessna 150/152s.

It's not that I was trying to get myself or anyone else killed, but it was thrilling and sometimes I can't help but take risks. It was important to me to produce competent pilots, and I never had an issue getting the little Thunder Hawk out of a spin.

The FAA has since ordered a fix of stall strips on the wings, and I believe it is allowed to be spun again.

Largely because of the spin characteristics, the Tomahawk has developed a bad reputation with some, but having a lot of hours in it, I always thought – and still think – it is a great little airplane.

One of the fringe benefits of being a flight instructor was dropping into airports for lunch or dinner if you were out late teaching night flying.

Just about every small airport has a café, and if time permitted, we'd stop to enjoy a leisurely lunch. Frequently the student would pick up the check. One of my favorite places while I was teaching navigation and radio work in the busy Southern California airspace was Meadowlark Field in Huntington Beach.

It was also good short field practice because of its short, narrow runway. At the little café, seating was on picnic tables over the worn lawn. Just a few miles from the beach, the weather always seemed good for outdoor dining.

Readers might remember some of the stories of Meadowlark Airport from my book, *Better Lucky Than Good*. Unfortunately, the land was worth more for housing and, thus, the airport is no longer there.

The little café at Meadowlark.

Another favorite was the El Rojo Baron at Riverside Airport, now just called the Riverside Airport Café. It was nice and close to Hemet, only about a thirty-minute flight.

Landing at various airports for lunch made us feel like jetsetters — only we were more like propsetters. No martinis or fine wines for us. We stuck with ham sandwiches and iced tea.

Back then, the little "Rancho" airport at Temecula was another place to drop in and walk across the street for lunch.

The single runway was right next to the hills and paralleled the ridgeline, causing the wind to dump off the hills to the runway at a ninety-degree angle. Rancho had a fierce reputation for crosswinds, so it was a great place to take my students to practice. It is now closed, and the nearby French Valley Airport serves the needs of that ever-growing community.

Try not to become a man of success.
Rather become a man of value.

~ Albert Einstein

Chapter 4
Movin' on up

Having started as a flight instructor in October, I'd been running the operation by myself for several months. Eventually the owner hired a secretary and a general manager to make it more than just a flight school but also a Piper Aircraft dealership and charter operation.

Norm Foster was the new manager and now my immediate boss. He was doing this just temporarily because his real job during the summer was as an air tanker pilot, flying on the fires for the state of California. He was one of those heroes of the sky.

It was now 1981. One January day Norm said, "I'm going to Santa Rosa in a few days to talk to them about a seat in an S-2 Tanker for the next season. Would you like to go along and see if they have a job for you?"

I said, "Yeah, absolutely." Then I hesitated and asked, "But how much time do they require?"

Norm said, "Not sure. I think about one thousand hours total time."

"Damn, I'm a little short of that."

He cocked his head with a sly smile and said, "Don't worry, a logbook tells only what you don't have. I'll vouch for you."

"Do you think they'd put me in a tanker?"

"Probably more like an 'Air Attack' job. Flying the spotter plane for the tankers."

"Sounds great. I'll take anything they've got to offer as long as it has wings."

"Even an angel?"

"Especially an angel." But then, thinking of Hells Angels, I said, "That depends on what kind."

***

The next week Norm and I climbed into the big, three-hundred-horsepower Piper Lance.

Because his IFR rating wasn't current and mine was, he said, "Why don't you drive?"

"My pleasure." I grinned.

As soon as I retracted the landing gear, I started a mild bank to the northwest. Contacting Los Angeles Center, I opened our IFR flight plan.

"Good morning LA Center, Piper five-five-four-four-foxtrot is with you off Hemet Ryan Field climbing through three thousand feet."

"Piper five-five-four-four-foxtrot, good morning, squawk 6261 and ident."

Tuning the transponder, I spun the dials to the required frequency and pushed the identification button.

"Piper four-four-foxtrot, radar contact, turn to three-three-five degrees, climb and maintain one-zero thousand, you're cleared direct Paradise."

We were on our way, wrapped in the loving arms of air traffic control, climbing to pass over March Air Force Base. We could look down and see B-52 bombers and KC-135 aerial refueling tankers parked on the ramp – on standby to go to war with the Soviet Union at a moment's notice.

The weather was the same old boring clear blue skies that California was famous for… except when it wasn't. With a lot of high mountains and a vast ocean alongside, smog, fog, and marine layers were a constant danger. Flying in this state could be as challenging as flying in Alaska, but not today.

We had a smooth flight in VFR conditions, but I had filed the IFR flight plan just for practice and to give us traffic separation in the busy Los Angeles basin.

The Lance was a sleek, modern, low-wing, six-seat aircraft with retractable landing gear. It had a three-hundred-horsepower engine with a constant-speed propeller and a cruising speed of one hundred and forty knots (one hundred and sixty-three miles per hour).

Flying it was a pleasure, especially after my little eighty-five horsepower Cessna 140, which was thirty-five years older. I couldn't afford to buy an airplane like this, nor could I afford to rent it. While I normally got paid to fly it on charter flights, right now Norm and I were borrowing it for this trip. I think he rigged the books to pay for the gas and flight time. Company business, you know.

Two hours and forty-two minutes later, after flying half the length of the state, we rolled the main wheels onto runway 32 at Santa Rosa, California.

As we taxied in, I was amazed. It was the off-season and it seemed like all the firefighting aircraft in the world were right there, parked wherever there was room: rows of Grumman S-2 tankers, huge four-engine Douglas DC-4s and DC-6s, and smaller Cessna O-2A spotter planes.

Lines of O-2As at Santa Rosa.

Parking on the ramp outside Sis-Q Flying Service, I set the parking brake. We unfolded ourselves from the cockpit and climbed off the wing. I pulled on a light jacket as we strolled across the tarmac and into the hangar. It was January – wintertime in Northern California. The sky was deep blue and lush green grass was everywhere that wasn't paved. It looked more like Ireland.

The company was named after Siskiyou County in Northern California. Its biggest claim to fame was Mount Shasta, a beautiful dormant volcano usually capped with snow all year round.

Sis-Q's chief pilot was Harry Chaffee, a husky man with short grey hair. We found him in the hangar talking with several mechanics. Seeing

Norm, he immediately walked over, extended his hand, and greeted him warmly with his gravelly voice.

"Well, I'll be damned. When did they let you out of jail?"

"Good to see you too, Harry." Norm chuckled.

"I'm glad you could stop by. I've been saving a seat for you."

"Where at and how much?" Norm asked.

"Columbia, the usual rate, like last year."

"You've got a deal."

Harry looked at me and said, "Who's your friend?"

"This is Dale. He works for me in Hemet. I think he's got a lot of talent, was wondering if you had a spot for him?"

Looking at Norm, Harry said, "Are you sure he's up for this? It can be dangerous."

"From what I know about him, he's been through a lot worse."

Harry stuck out his hand, and I struggled to return his firm grip. He said, "I'm pleased to meet you. How would you like to fly one of our Air Attacks?"

"I'd be happy to."

"It pays seven hundred dollars a month and seven dollars per flight hour on dispatches. No pay for ferry flights. Depending on the fire season, it should last about four and a half months."

"Sounds good to me. I'll take it."

"Welcome aboard, I'm glad to have you."

Earlier in the day, after taking off from Hemet, Norm and I had been cleared direct to Paradise VOR, near Riverside Airport. Now I was thinking, 'Maybe this is paradise…'

Being offered a job flying on forest fires for the California Department of Forestry (contracted through Sis-Q Flying Service), I thought to myself, 'This flying business just keeps getting better and better.'

Or… perhaps the line from "Hotel California: *This could be heaven, or this could be hell.*"

You know, Hobbes, some days even my lucky rocket ship underpants don't help.

~ Bill Watterson

Chapter 5
Working for a living

Back in Hemet, I continued working with my students with a new confidence. I had a more exciting job on the horizon, but the fire season wouldn't be for several more months.

Though I didn't necessarily need it, I studied for my instrument instructor's rating: the lofty CFII. Getting more qualified was almost an obsession. When I wasn't flying or working with a student, or after work in the evenings, I'd be at my desk studying for the FAA written test, which was required before the flight check. Sometimes I'd fly with Curt to practice the instrument approaches, and as I got closer to taking the test, I flew with the highly experienced instructors at Riverside Air Service.

One day I was going out with two ladies to do some IFR instruction during VFR conditions. One would fly while the other watched from the back seat. About an hour was sufficient before fatigue set in. IFR training could be grueling.

We'd land, relax, and have lunch at one of the many airport restaurants in the Southern California area. When we got back in the air, they'd switch places, more training would ensue, and we'd end up back at Hemet.

On this particular day, after the ground briefing, we were parked in a row of aircraft and the student named Debbie had just started the engine. She was in the left seat and, as the instructor, I was in the right.

Jeri was in the back seat. She owned the airplane, a Piper Cherokee Warrior – a nice little four-seater with a one-hundred-sixty horsepower engine. In some ways, it was the perfect private airplane. But then everyone had their own opinion about that.

There was no tower or ground control. Hemet was an "uncontrolled field," so all aircraft were on their own to announce their location and intentions to other aircraft.

Pulling out of the parking space, we made a left turn to taxi toward the runway. We were still in the ramp area with rows of airplanes parked on either side of us.

As soon as we could see ahead, I noticed an aircraft taxiing toward us. No one had called on the radio, so I was surprised to see anyone moving on the airport.

I told Debbie to stop, hold her position, and wait to see what this guy was going to do.

As the aircraft got closer, I could see it was a small aerobatic "Pitts" biplane.

Many conventional aircraft – meaning a taildragger like this biplane – sit with their tail down and their nose in the air. The pilot needs to do "S-turns," swerving back and forth to see ahead. In that Pitts, if you don't do that, it's impossible to see what's in front of you.

I said to Debbie, "Hold here. Let's see what he's gonna do. Maybe he'll turn left at the end of the hangar."

She said, "He sure is going fast."

"Yeah, too fast."

He didn't turn at the end of the hangar. Instead, he came barreling straight at us.

Grabbing the microphone from its holder, I glanced at the frequency to make sure we were on Unicom, then said, "Pitts biplane at Hemet, are you on frequency?"

No answer!

I said, "He's not S-turning."

Then, "I don't think he sees us."

He came charging straight down the taxiway into the parking ramp, never S-turning to see ahead and not slowing down.

Into the microphone, I almost shouted, "Pitts biplane at Hemet…"

It was too late. Feeling helpless, with nothing more to do, I yelled for the ladies to brace themselves as the biplane drove straight into us with a sickening crunch.

His nose contacted just right of our nose, then glanced off as his propeller sliced its way up the right side of the Warrior's engine cowling, cutting through the thin aluminum and leaving gashes like the gills of a shark until the propeller stopped inches from my right foot.

Upon impact, as his plane slammed forward, his tail came up, and no more than four feet away I saw the surprised look on his face. Of course, he had no idea we were there.

The engine had stopped immediately on impact. I reached for the mixture to shut off the fuel, hoping no fuel lines had been cut that could start a fire. I couldn't believe this guy would drive right into us without looking where he was going.

I asked my students, "Are you okay?"

"Yes," they responded in shaky voices.

"Turn off the ignition and set the parking brake. Let's get out of here," I said.

As we were climbing off the wing, the guy was getting out of his open cockpit. He was about in his mid-thirties and had a sheepish look on his face.

I walked toward him as he stepped to the ground. He turned to me and said, "Well, I guess it's nobody's fault, really."

Shocked and almost speechless, I said, "We've been sitting here parked, watching you come up the taxiway. You never S-turned once to see where you were going. I tried to call you on the radio. Don't give me that. This is entirely *your* fault."

He said, "My radio's not working."

"All the more reason to watch where you're going."

Then he said, "Let's just let the insurance companies take care of it. We don't need to get the FAA involved."

"I don't care about the FAA. I just want to know that your insurance will fix this airplane."

I realized I was shaking with anger. Not so many years ago I would have taken it out on this guy with my fists. Maybe I *was* making progress.

He just turned and walked away as I headed to the flight office to let them know what had happened.

A couple of days later I found out more about this guy when I was confronted by my boss, Jill, who owned the flight school/Piper dealership.

With her hands on her hips, she said, "I see you met Hal the other day, the guy in the Pitts."

"Unfortunately. Why, you know him?"

"Yeah, he's a good friend of mine. What the hell is wrong with you pulling out in front of him like that?"

Taken aback, I almost laughed in her face. Instead, I said, "Is that what he told you? He's lying, and I have two other witnesses who will verify what happened. Let's have the FAA sort it out in an accident report."

Suddenly her tone changed as she tried to protect him. "No, wait, there's no need for that. I'll make sure his insurance takes care of it."

It turned out her careless friend Hal was a flight engineer for Trans World Airlines. He was afraid of getting the FAA involved and having an accident on his record. That could affect his job.

The Warrior was repaired and back in the air, but it took about six months – six months of lost flight training for Jeri and Debbie. It amazed me that a professional pilot could be so careless.

By the second of May, after continued training, I took my check ride for my instrument flight instructor's rating, my CFII. I felt more highly qualified than I'd ever been. But I never really got to use it.

Fire season was about to start. On May 28, Sis-Q wanted me in Santa Rosa to start the next phase of my flying career. I made arrangements for Curt to take over with my students, and then I quit my first flying job.

Dream lofty dreams, and as you dream, so shall you become.
~James Allen

Chapter 6
Smoke gets in your eyes ~ The Platters

I drove my '77 Pontiac Le Mans over the Gorman Pass into the San Joaquin Valley. I traveled north up Highway 99 and finally turned right at the familiar city of Modesto, climbing into the foothills of the Sierra Nevada mountains. They were roads I had traveled many times just years before on a motorcycle. Some readers have ridden those roads with me.

I arrived at the small, old Forty-Niner mining town of Columbia, just north of Sonora. Norm had arranged to rent a single-wide mobile home with bedrooms at either end. It was in a park next to the airport where we'd be based. We'd be sharing the trailer, and the ride to work was five minutes.

Working on fires is always seasonal. For this part of California, that means from June through the end of September. The fire season lasts longer down south.

Each CDF base for the California Department of Forestry (today called Cal Fire) had a complement of two S2-F air tankers and one Air Attack spotter. Norm had a lot of experience. He'd be in Tanker 76. Shortly after our arrival, we met with Jim Eakin, who'd be flying Tanker 77.

Jim was new to flying tankers on fires, but you wouldn't have known it, as he was almost as good as Norm. He'd flown for Air America, the secret CIA air force in Vietnam, Laos, Thailand, and Cambodia during the war there. Risky flying. To him, fires were nothing.

The next day a twin-engine Cessna 402 showed up from Sis-Q and flew the three of us to Santa Rosa to pick up our airplanes for the season.

The instructor who checked me out was a young guy named Ted Bell. For two and a half hours we did single-engine work, stalls, touch-and-go landings, and single-engine go-arounds. Plus, he taught me to do "map drops," in which your passenger, the Air Attack captain or ranger, would draw a map for the ground commander and you'd deliver it to him. It was a little mini-bombing mission, and that was always fun.

Ted had been a schoolteacher, but he quit that profession because he wanted more than anything to be a tanker pilot. He was a great guy, and we were friends for several years.

After the training flight, there was a short check ride with Blaine Moore, the battalion chief for the Sonoma Air Attack Base. I was declared good to go.

Next, I took up the aircraft I'd be flying for the summer to check it out. According to my logbook, I declared an emergency because of the landing gear. I don't remember the details – probably no down and locked indication. The tower rolled the fire trucks and emergency equipment, but the landing was normal.

When we were ready, Norm, Jim, and I flew our respective airplanes back to Columbia to start the fire season.

During the one-hour-and-twenty-minute flight, I noticed a film of oil was forming on the windshield – a leak from the front engine.

On the ground in Columbia, I called the Sis-Q maintenance office at Santa Rosa. Harry answered. When I told him about the oil on the windshield, he said, "It's probably the new prop seals. Let's just keep an eye on it. They may seat-in and it'll be okay."

The S2s that Norm and Jim would be flying were big old Navy airplanes that had flown off aircraft carriers when they were used as submarine trackers. Having been converted into tankers to fight fires, they were powered by two big, snarling radial engines – the same kind of motor that powered most airplanes during World War II.

They had charisma, with those engines sounding like giant flying Harley-Davidsons, or warbirds, which they actually were. Still fighting a war after all these years, only against fires.

The Navy had flown them with two pilots. The California Department of Forestry, or CDF, operated them with just one.

My new ride was N468DF, "Air Attack 440," and that was my radio callsign. It was a Cessna O-2A, which is a military version of the civilian Cessna 337. They had formerly belonged to the U.S. Air Force and had two 210-horsepower engines with one motor on the front of the fuselage and one on the back between twin booms that held the tail assembly.

A fleet of them was based at different locations around the state. These particular airplanes had flown in Vietnam as "Forward Air Controllers," or FACs, calling out targets for air strikes from fighter-bombers or artillery.

They'd also carried rockets, flares, and even sometimes 7.62 mini-guns under their wings. On top of the instrument panel in front of me was a platform that had once held a gun site. In the back were radio racks that had held big UHF radios for the Air Force, and along one bulkhead were clamps to hold M-16s.

So, technically, it was a warbird too, only without the muscular roar of a big radial or inline Merlin engine.

In Vietnam, it was dangerous work and these O-2s still bore patches in the skin from bullet holes. One of the Sis-Q mechanics told me that, according to his records, he had worked on these very same airplanes at Tan-Son-Nhut air base outside Saigon.

I was thrilled to have this job, and although I liked the O-2, I envied the Tanker pilots, not only for the big S-2s they flew but also for their heroic mission of putting out fires. They also made a lot more money.

I couldn't wait to get out and fly on some missions, which didn't take long.

Finally on station at Columbia, my first dispatch wasn't a fire. It was to recon near Angles Camp, which was hosting a rock concert. I suppose they were worried about campfires getting out of control.

I didn't mention to CDF Fire Captain Sutton, who was flying with me, that ten years ago I'd been at those same fairgrounds with my club brothers, attending the annual Frog Jump and expecting trouble from other motorcycle clubs.

But I didn't have time to reminisce. I had a job to do. We flew only a little over an hour, and when we got back on the ground, I had to clean the oil off the windshield. Those seals still hadn't "seated-in."

The Air Attack base at Columbia was a great place to work, well-kept with tall pine trees all around and mowed lawns like in a park. There was a large Quonset hut and a control tower about four stories high. It was run by the California Department of Forestry, which we were contracted to by Sis-Q.

Half the Quonset hut comprised the pilots' ready room to hang out in, with a kitchen, a small television, and, in case we wanted to sleep, old metal G.I. bunk beds. Unlike the "Helitack" firefighters based there, we weren't required to work when we weren't flying.

The back half of the Quonset hut was reserved for a workshop, maintenance, and a weight room that I utilized almost every day.

There was a lot of radio traffic on loudspeakers all over the base. Most of the traffic was routine, but you could usually tell if something was brewing and you might be going out.

When the alarm went off for aircraft to be sent out, we'd run to the flightline. It always reminded me of those old films from World War II in which the pilots would "scramble," running for their planes and getting airborne as quickly as possible.

I thought it was great fun and exciting. Our aircraft were parked on a ramp at the north end of the main runway. We'd jump in and fire up the engines, then do a brief radio check before the short taxi to runway 17.

We always used 17 for takeoff no matter what the wind was. It was slightly downhill. Like Hemet, Columbia was an uncontrolled field, so we broadcast our intentions on the radio to all aircraft in the area. Most of the time, when other pilots heard that firefighting aircraft wanted to take off or land, they'd give us the runway.

The flight line at Columbia, 1981.

My passenger was usually Ranger Jerry Watson. He was the head of the Air Attack base and had many years of experience fighting fires from the ground and the air.

He wasn't a pilot, though. My job was to give him an aerial platform from which to view the fire. He called the shots for the tankers and fed information to the firefighters on the ground, if there were any.

I didn't have to know anything about fighting fires. My job was to put the airplane where the Ranger wanted it. That was usually fifteen hundred feet above the incident, circling in a right-hand turn so he could see out the right window.

Some days my passenger would be his second-in-command, Bob Sutton.

Captain Sutton was an easy-going guy and fun to fly with. Ranger Watson was all business and didn't laugh much. If he did, it was more sardonic or caustic. He looked about sixty years old, although I never asked him. However, he was tolerant of me being a new guy, and I did my best to do the job right and keep us safe. I was proud to be working with such professionals.

I was totally gung-ho and didn't care how long the missions lasted. On our second dispatch, with Captain Sutton again, I'd had the long-range wing tanks filled – something Ranger Watson later forbade for good reason, which I will explain later.

Bob and I flew for almost seven hours on a large fast-moving grass fire by the Rancho Seco nuclear plant near Sacramento. It was being pushed by thirty-mile-per-hour winds and burned fifteen thousand acres.

Remember that leaking front propeller seal that was blowing oil back onto the windshield? After almost seven hours of flying through the smoke and ash in the air from the fire, the windshield was now completely brown. We couldn't see straight ahead.

We could see out the sides, however, and I could navigate by instruments. Bob kept asking me, "Are you going to be able to land this thing?"

Always up for a challenge, I assured him, "Sure, no problem."

Finally, we were relieved by another air attack from Hollister and headed back to Columbia. On final approach, I side-slipped us down to the runway, looking out my left window.

In the flare, I straightened the nose and used my peripheral vision to touch down and keep us on the center line. All that tail dragger time in the past came in handy.

Bob must have mentioned the situation to Ranger Watson, who probably called Sis-Q. The next day Harry called and told me to bring 440 to Santa Rosa. They'd fix the problem. When I got there, instead of putting me in a hotel room, Harry took me to his home and put me in a spare room. I was never sure if he'd taken a liking to me or if the company's owner was too cheap to pay for a hotel room.

Maybe it was both. This wouldn't be the last time I stayed at his house.

Among the lucky, you are the chosen one.

~A fortune cookie I had once

Chapter 7
Flying combat against a fiery enemy

A typical dispatch went something like this: We received instructions on heading and distance, which was frequently unnecessary. Once airborne, if the fire was within fifty miles, you could see the smoke.

Because the tankers were faster than my O-2, they'd usually arrive first. They'd go into a left-hand orbit around the fire at one thousand feet and start reporting what they saw. As the senior tanker pilot, Norm would do the talking.

Norm: "Air Attack Four Four Zero, Tanker seven six."

Ranger Watson: "Go ahead, Seven-Six, what have you got?"

"Brush and grass in relatively flat terrain, about two acres so far, moving fast with the wind, no structures involved, but several houses and barns are downwind and in danger."

"How close to the structures?"

"About a mile at this time."

Jerry looked at me and said, "How long?"

With the throttles at maximum manifold pressure, I replied, "Five minutes."

"Roger, Seven-Six, we're five out, stand by."

On another radio, Watson called Columbia base: "Columbia, Four Four Oh."

"Go ahead, Four Four Zero."

"Start Helitack on the way."

"Roger that."

Contrary to popular belief, air tankers don't normally put out fires. They spread a retardant ahead of the fire to keep more fuel from igniting. Thus, they try to starve the fire of fuel and stop the spread.

Just like in a real war, you can't win it from the air. You can only slow down the enemy so the ground troops can engage it head-on.

The real work of putting out the fire was the job of the firefighters on the ground. Helitack crews are a small group of elite and very fit young men and sometimes women. They're dropped off by helicopter at the head of the fire to try to stop it.

If a water source was available, the helicopter would deploy a bucket and fight the fire with water drops. This augmented what the ground crews and tankers were doing: a three-pronged attack.

Arriving over the fire at fifteen hundred feet, I pulled back the throttles as I rolled into a tight right-hand orbit, bleeding off airspeed with the turn.

We orbited right so Jerry could see out the right-side window. Meanwhile, the tankers at one thousand feet orbited left so the pilots could look down from their side window. When helicopters were on the scene, they stayed at five hundred and below.

By now the fire had advanced to within half a mile from the houses and barns. No ground crews were on the scene yet and there were no accessible roads.

Ranger Watson went into action: "Tanker Seven-Six, I want you to give me two doors in trail along that fence line at the head of the fire. Tanker Seven-Seven, follow him and put two doors just to the right of his drop. Both of you come around and do it again, laying a path between the fire and those structures."

"Tanker Seven-Six, Roger that."

"Seven-Seven copies."

Each door in the belly of the S-2s held two hundred gallons of Phos-Chek retardant, so each one could drop a total of eight hundred gallons in increments of two hundred, four hundred, or all eight hundred at once.

I watched as the bombers swept in, diving close to the ground with long crimson streaks billowing out from their bellies onto the golden grass. It was an awesome aerial ballet, and I was thrilled to be a part of it.

Once the drops were made, Watson radioed, "Good job. Both of you return to base and bring us another load."

"Roger, load and return."

"Copy that."

As I watched them climb and bank back to the east, I desperately wanted to be flying one of those awesome aircraft.

Being satisfied has always been difficult for me. Whatever success I achieved, I wanted more. There was always something better to aspire to. Luckily, in aviation, there are always higher goals to reach; there is always another brass ring.

This kind of operation is an example of what we did every day, sometimes several times a day on smaller fires. Sometimes on a big fire – and there were many of those – we'd fly on the same fire two or three days in a row.

There were times when Ranger Watson and I got sent to check out smoke to see if the tankers were needed. We might get there and find ground crews already on the scene, and the ground boss would ask for advice from the airborne Ranger. On any fire, the ground boss was always in charge.

At other times Jerry and I were put on patrol high up over the Sierras. We'd look for smoke after thunderstorms had come through the night before and there had been numerous lightning strikes.

Those patrols were great, cruising over the beautiful high Sierras. Sometimes we'd drop down low to investigate any signs of smoke. Many times, we spotted a small fire before it grew out of control and directed in ground crews. Other times it was just someone's campfire.

If a fire was growing in a remote location and no ground crews had gotten there, Ranger Watson would bring in the tankers and the Helitack crew to get a head start on the blaze.

It was common for the tankers and the Air Attack to be dispatched to other parts of the state to help out with a big fire.

A real flying job. The author with Air Attack 440 at Columbia Base. The Quonset hut is at the upper left.

Be careful what you wish for.

~Unknown

Chapter 8
Are we having fun yet?

"**S**anta Rosa Tower, Air Attack Four Four Zero is five miles east inbound with information Zulu."

"Roger, Air Attack Four Four Zero, proceed inbound. Runway two-zero is recommended, but you can have whatever you need."

Information Zulu said the airport was closed. "Emergency in Progress," read the ATIS. But it wasn't closed for us. We *were* the emergency.

Circling the Santa Rosa airport at one thousand feet, Ranger Watson and I were in trouble. The O-2's landing gear was stuck halfway down. Upon our return to Columbia from a false alarm over an hour ago, the wheels wouldn't extend before landing.

I'd already made a couple of low passes down the runway so the maintenance people could see the problem.

We had plenty of gas, so we circled to burn off fuel. We didn't want to feed a fire if things didn't go well.

On the flight over I'd tried the emergency procedure several times. It consisted of pumping a small handle on the floor connected to a hydraulic pump to operate the landing gear in whatever direction the gear selector was positioned. In this case, the handle was down and the procedure hadn't worked.

At some point, we'd have to land, wheels or no wheels. The fuel would last only so long and it was getting late. We didn't want to do this in the dark.

An example of a 337 with the gear hanging down.

With the gear hanging halfway down, I wasn't confident about landing. I was afraid it would tip the airplane on its side, where a wingtip would dig in and we could cartwheel and roll into a ball. The possibility of fire was very real, but I didn't want to tell this to Jerry Watson.

I gave him a briefing on what to expect: "I'm not sure what will happen when we touch down, but when the airplane comes to a stop, get yourself out as quickly as possible. Don't worry about me. If I can't get out, that's what the rescue crews are here for."

The only door to get in and out was on his side of the aircraft.

Jerry's expression was grim. He just nodded. He wasn't having fun.

Just then Harry called me on the radio and said, "The emergency crews are ready. Have you tried to put the gear up?"

"No, I've only tried pumping them down."

"Neil Emery, our head mechanic, is suggesting you try to put them up."

"Okay, can't hurt. Let's see what happens."

Selecting the landing gear handle to the up position, I reached down and started pumping on the little handle. To my surprise, the three red lights on the instrument panel went out.

Another flight down the runway at low altitude confirmed that not only were the wheels now up, but the gear doors were also closed.

Elated, I pushed the throttles up and climbed back to five hundred feet to go around the pattern again. I knew that with a clean belly, the airplane would slide smoothly upon landing and almost certainly stay upright.

A shot of my aircraft, N468DF, with the gear up.

The radio crackled again and Harry said, "Do you want to try to put them down again? It's up to you."

"No, I don't want to get back into the same situation with them halfway down. I'll just bring her in this way."

"Okay, that's fine. Don't worry about the props hitting."

"Roger that."

With the propellers turning, they'd certainly contact the runway with the airplane on its belly. That would not only ruin the props but also hurt the engines. Damage and cost would be extensive.

Jerry wanted to know if they were going to foam the runway. I asked.

The answer was, "No, we don't do that anymore."

I said, "Okay."

When Harry told me that he wasn't worried about the propellers hitting, it meant he didn't care about the damage or the cost. He just wanted us to get on the ground safely.

I had other ideas. The O-2 had an engine in the front and one in the back. I could see the front propeller but not the back one.

With the fire trucks standing by, the tower cleared me to land. On the downwind leg I pulled back the three levers, the throttle, the propeller control to feather it, and then the fuel lever to shut down the front engine.

A shudder went through the airframe, and I watched the propeller stop in front of my face. I dropped a notch of flaps as we slowed and added power to the rear engine. Then I rolled in some nose-up trim to keep the airplane level.

The prop was almost vertical so one blade would contact the runway. I bumped the starter button to bring it horizontal, such that neither blade would touch. I'd save at least one engine.

Operating on only the back engine, I had a dry throat as I turned for our final approach to runway two-zero. I nosed down, diving at the ground, and pulled the rear throttle back as we headed for the end of the runway. Just as we crossed the threshold at fifty feet in the air, I pulled back the other two levers and chopped the rear engine too.

Because of its position on the fuselage, I was pretty sure the prop wouldn't hit. We were now committed and weren't going to be needing it. Besides, I wanted that fuel shut off.

The airframe shuddered again, and the silence was eerie. The only noise was the wind, which got quieter as the speed bled off. It was disturbing. Pilots don't like quiet.

As the O-2 slowed, I started easing back on the yoke to bring the nose up into a flare, holding us off the asphalt runway. I wanted to be going as slow as possible when we touched down.

Through the deafening silence, I heard a dragging sound. Like the old curb finders on cars, the VHF radio antennas on the belly of the airplane started touching the runway.

I knew I was within one foot. The dragging got louder until the back of the belly of the airplane contacted the runway.

The scraping became very loud as the nose plopped down and we started sliding.

To my surprise, I had complete rudder control and was able to keep the airplane straight down the centerline. My ability to steer continued until we slowed to about twenty knots. Even with full right rudder, the nose pointed slightly to the left as we came to a complete stop, still sitting on the centerline and right next to one of the fire trucks.

Taking what felt like my first breath in five minutes, I wiped my sweaty palms on my jeans and turned to my right with a big smile to tell Jerry the obvious: "We made it."

However, I found the seat empty, the door open, and his headset swinging back and forth, hanging from its coiled wire.

I'd forgotten to tell him we'd be fine, with a smooth, clean belly to land on.

The infamous gear-up landing. Santa Rosa airport, August 4, 1981.

***

The Cessna 0-2A had an interesting addition to its design. Built to fly in combat, it was designed to take small arms fire from the ground while doing its low and slow job as a forward air controller.

It had two raised rails on the belly with aluminum strips riveted on, made for this very purpose. They were like runners on a sled, made from aluminum so they wouldn't spark when sliding along a runway, and I knew they were there. Once I got the gear back up, I was confident we'd be able to land on those skids.

I wandered around the runway in a daze, accepting congratulations, often from people I didn't know. Some Sis-Q mechanics went to work fixing the broken hydraulic line while another brought out a truck with an A-frame crane. After adding more hydraulic fluid, they lifted the 0-2 off the ground.

After replacing the hydraulic fluid, they used the emergency handle to pump the gear down. Just as it locked into place, the aluminum handle broke off. I had stressed it by pumping so hard, over and over to try to get the gear down, that it had weakened, cracked, and finally given out. If it had broken while we were in the air, I never would have gotten the wheels up and had that smooth belly to land on.

Johnny, the mechanic, stood there holding the broken lever in his hand. He started laughing. The rest of us laughed too. *Better lucky than good.*

With the battery switch on, three green lights appeared on the panel. A mechanic fired up the front engine and taxied it back to the hangar.

The Department of Forestry put Ranger Watson in a hotel for the night. However, because I wasn't working a fire, that wasn't in my contract. So, once again, Harry took me home to his house for the night.

After dinner, we shared a couple of glasses of whisky before bed, talking about the day's events. It made me feel almost like I had a new family.

***

The next morning, after breakfast with his family, we were back at the hangar by ten o'clock. They were still working on my airplane. The four radio antennas and a red rotating beacon on the belly had been torn off on the landing and had already been replaced. A new handle for the emergency pump had been installed too.

Harry and I went to hang out in the pilots' ready room for the Sonoma base.

One of the crew there was the battalion chief for the Sonoma base: Ranger Blaine Moore. I knew him from when he'd given me my check ride before the season started. A young lady named Barbara was the Air Attack pilot at Santa Rosa that year. She was a cute, tiny redhead.

While we sat around chatting and drinking coffee, the alarm went off for the Air Attack to be dispatched to a fire. Blaine surprised me when he looked at Barbara and said, "How about if we put Dale on this flight?"

She smiled and said, "Fine by me. I'll just take it easy here."

They both looked at me. I shrugged and said, "Let's go."

We trotted out to where the AA140 sat near the tankers and jumped in. It was identical to mine.

When we climbed out on our assigned heading, it felt different because of the much lower density altitude at Santa Rosa. The airplane seemed to perform better.

Upon our arrival at the location of the fire fifteen minutes later, we saw that a ground crew was already on the scene. They had it under control, so we turned back to base.

We were gone for only half an hour. I found out later that Barbara had gotten paid for my flight because it was her airplane. That meant I lost three dollars and fifty cents of flight pay. I didn't squawk about it.

Afterward, I wondered if Blaine had wanted to ride with me to see if I was rattled after the gear-up landing the day before. I wasn't, but I didn't ask.

Back in the hangar, I checked on the progress on my airplane. Dave, one of the mechanics and a friend of mine, said, "I can't believe how little damage was done to this thing. They should give you a raise."

I said, "Harry said it was considered a ferry flight, and I don't get paid for ferry flights."

He shook his head and walked away.

The aluminum shoes on the skids – the ones I'd ground down the day before – had been replicated and were riveted back on the runners. By noon, Jerry and I were back in the air, returning to Columbia to get back to work.

***

On August 10, 1981, the Director of Aviation and Fire Management for the U.S. Forest Service put out a memo to all forest supervisors and zone aviation officers, explaining what happened and giving Ranger Watson and me a "well done." I've included that memo in the back of this book.

Never give up, never quit, fly it till the end.
~Chuck Aaron

Chapter 9
A busy week

The foothills of the Sierra Nevada mountains compose some of the most beautiful countryside in the state of California. To me, it seemed an almost idyllic lifestyle – escaping the summer heat of the San Joaquin Valley without the extreme cold and snow of the high country in the winter.

It is also some of the most dangerous countryside when it comes to the fires that happen every year. Sometimes they are more numerous and intense, but every year sees them nonetheless.

I have to wonder: Without the efforts of the California Department of Forestry, would it even be possible to live there, lacking protection from that all-consuming fire-breathing dragon, the forest fire?

***

Three days after the gear-up landing, we were dispatched to a very hot fire called the Buchanan Fire. We flew on it for almost six hours that day and were back at it early the next morning. It was now burning toward the little town of Tuolumne, less than ten miles from Columbia.

It was one of those bad fires in difficult terrain with lots of fuel. When we arrived on the scene, Jerry started calling in reinforcements of other tankers from around the state. This would be a big one.

There were high ridges covered with brush-like scrub oak and various large trees along with the dry California "golden" grass. It was all tinder-dry and ready to explode into flames – which it was doing with enthusiasm. A stiff breeze was happy to help.

The canyons were steep along the north fork of the Tuolumne River. It was tough work, and a lot of homes were in the fire's path. The town was being evacuated, and the roads were clogged with residents trying to leave and fire trucks trying to come in. Firefighters on the ground were working hard in the hot, dry conditions.

We flew for almost six hours that day. When we landed back at Columbia, S-2 tankers from other parts of the state were parked all over the ramp. Pilots from out of town piled into the cars of local pilots and firefighters and headed into Sonora seeking dinner and refreshments.

If not for the dreaded threat of the nearby fire, it would have seemed almost like a party – a chance to hang out with friends and fellow pilots. The stories, jokes, and lies got almost as thick as the smoke hanging over the town. It didn't last long, as around ten o'clock we were all tired and knew we'd be back at it in the morning. We dropped off the out-of-town pilots at their motels and Norm and I retired to our single-wide mobile home.

The next morning the retardant loading crews were already busy filling one S-2 after another. It was one of those combat/wartime atmospheres in which everyone was doing their best to fight the enemy. That was what it felt like, and I was excited to be part of it.

We ate a hurried breakfast at the Egg Cellar Café near Columbia Airport. Soon after, Jerry Watson and I were circling the worst location, which was getting the most attention from the tankers. With the sun coming up and heating the ground, the wind was increasing and the gains the ground crews had made overnight were being lost. The fight was back on.

One after another, tankers swooped in, dispensing their crimson cargo ahead of the fire, trying to stop its advance. However, the stubborn wind-driven flames and embers kept leaping over the retardant lines and the hand lines cut by the ground crews, crossing ridgelines and hopping across canyons to start anew. The flames crept closer to the town of Tuolumne.

A couple of hours into this, on day two, the radio seemed to crackle with electricity when we heard the excited voice of a firefighter on the ground say, "There's a helicopter going down… It just crashed!"

Ranger Watson said into the radio, "Four Oh Four, how do you read?"

No answer. It was the only helicopter working this fire.

I switched to the discreet VHF pilot-to-pilot frequency. "George, are you there?"

No answer.

Jerry and I looked at each other with dread in our eyes. We didn't know what had happened, as there were no details. They were all our friends. We worked together every day and practically lived together. Who was on board? How many? Were firefighters on board? Which captain was working that day? Were they okay? Were they all dead? It was so frustrating… We didn't know.

It was difficult to focus on our jobs as that sick feeling settled into our stomachs, into our whole beings – the thought that we might have lost not just one or two friends but a whole bunch of them.

We forced ourselves to focus on the job at hand and got back to business. People were depending on us: the tanker pilots, the firefighters on the ground, the people who lived below us.

Only later, after we got on the ground, did we find out what happened.

***

George Johnson looked down through the plexiglass bubble between his bare feet on the rudder pedals of the Bell 206 Jet Ranger helicopter as he held his hover while the Helitack crew on the ground filled his bucket for the next drop.

George always flew barefoot. He did everything barefoot. It might have been an old habit because of the "trench foot" so common in Vietnam, where he'd been a helicopter pilot. His feet were probably harder than the toughest leather boots, and he hated wearing shoes. I doubt he attended enough dinner parties where he'd need them.

When the ground crew hand signaled the bucket was full, George pulled up the collective as he rolled on the throttle. Easing the cyclic forward to put the nose down, he steered back toward the head of the fire, where he'd been making his drops.

He'd been working on the edge of town, the fire was that close, and hadn't gone far when he felt that literally sinking feeling as the engine wound down.

"Engine failure" went through his mind as he automatically dropped the collective, rolled off the throttle, and pulled the nose slightly up to keep the rotors turning while he searched for a place to land.

Keeping those rotors turning was the only thing keeping him in the air and under control and alive. Without that lift, the helicopter would have the flying characteristics of a piano.

As he punched off the load of water, he looked toward the pasture next to Tuolumne Road. He'd been keeping it in mind in case this happened. It was an old habit.

In an autorotation, you had control to steer, but it was all downhill. If you could find a flat spot to land, you'd be okay.

The little pasture next to the road was in range. No problem. As he glided toward it, he knew he'd make it. Then he saw the horses.

Landing on top of horses in a stricken helicopter didn't seem like a good idea. It wouldn't be good for the helicopter or the horses. Both would be damaged beyond repair. Besides, he liked horses.

Beyond the pasture was a cemetery. What a perfect place for a crash landing! If you didn't make it, you were all set.

With laser focus, George watched his rotor speed deteriorate as he pulled up the nose to stretch his glide over the horses and oak trees.

The airspeed deteriorated. The rotor speed deteriorated. He was out of options, out of ideas, and out of luck.

At about ten feet above the ground, where he wanted to push the nose over to accomplish a good emergency landing, the helicopter ran out of flying speed and plummeted to the ground with a shuddering crash.

***

It was Captain Gene Strand's day to work with the ground crew. He and the Helitack crew had been dropped off in a steep canyon. Gene directed his crew to cut fire break after fire break, but each time the line got jumped by embers causing spot fires behind their line. They'd grab their gear and race back downwind to start all over again.

It was hot, grueling work. It was also just another day on the job. They were all used to it. That was what it was to be a ground crew, to be "Helitack."

Suddenly, on his radio, Gene heard, "There's a helicopter going down… It just crashed!"

Gene knew George was the only helicopter on the fire. A chill went down his spine as he shouted to Don Stone, "You're in charge," and started running uphill to where trucks were parked.

Gene and George were close friends and flew together almost every day. They were as much a team as the firefighters themselves.

Seeing an unused vehicle, Gene shouted to one of the firefighters to drive as he jumped into a CDF pickup truck.

"Take me to the crash site."

"What crash site?"

"The helicopter that just went down!"

"What helicopter?"

The firefighter started the engine and dropped the gearshift into drive. Dust and gravel boiled off the rear wheels as he stomped on the gas.

Shouting into his radio, Gene asked, "Where is the crash site?"

The answer was, "At the cemetery."

Shaking his head at the irony, Gene told his driver, "Head up Tuolumne Road North."

Into his radio, Gene asked, "What's the status of the pilot?"

"He is slumped over in his seat and isn't moving."

Gene swore under his breath and shook his head, fearing the worst. He told his driver, "Step on it, will ya?"

***

Skidding to a halt in front of the cemetery, Gene bailed out and ran through the oak trees and tombstones. Soon he saw the wreckage of the Bell 206. The skids were flattened out and the belly of the helo was sitting on the ground. It had hit so hard, the rotor blades had flexed down and chopped off the tail boom.

George was calmly leaning against the fuselage of the destroyed helicopter, smoking his one cigarette of the day. It seemed like a good time.

Gene ran up asking, "Are you okay?"

George said, "Sure, I'm fine."

"What the hell? They said on the radio you were slumped over in your seat, not moving."

George chuckled and said, "Oh, I was trying to find my boots under my seat. I didn't want to get in trouble in case someone saw me flying barefoot."

Gene burst out laughing with relief. George laughed too.

It has been said that "Joy is the sudden cessation of great pain."

Certainly, emotional as well as physical.

Then George turned serious and said, "Ya know, about fifteen minutes before this happened, we'd done a recon of the fire with three CDF people on board. We were flying over that deep canyon. If the engine had quit then, I'm afraid it could have been very bad."

Gene said, "Looks like you really got lucky."

George shrugged. "You just never know in this business."

***

Jerry and I flew for seven and a half hours that day, even while being relieved several times by other Air Attack teams.

On the third day we did an hour and a half recon of the Buchanan Fire. The ground crews had it mostly under control. It was a great relief to know that we – a very large collective of air assets and ground crews – had stopped it and saved the town from being destroyed.

The very next day we had another memorable incident.

Flying on fires was exciting and rewarding. We frequently saved people's homes and, sometimes, their lives. Often it was firefighters who were caught in a bad spot, making drops right on top of them. The movie *Always* with Richard Dreyfuss centered around aerial firefighting and depicted a scene just like that.

One of the most memorable fires wasn't that big, but it happened at the edge of the town of Sonora, about only two miles from the end of the runway.

Pushed by high winds, the fire was fed by a lot of fuel, with trees and scrub oak. It quickly threatened homes and the town itself, which had many vulnerable old wooden buildings. For once the Ranger and I were on the scene first.

Taking off on runway 17, and climbing only a couple of hundred feet, the tankers had barely put up their wheels when they turned toward town and made their drops. Then, banking hard, they turned back to land in the opposite direction on runway 35. The engines weren't shut down, as the loading crews were kept busy filling the planes, one after the other.

On one of our circles around the fire, I noticed flames racing across a yard, toward a house against whose side brush was growing. I pointed it out to Ranger Watson.

Tanker 76 had just come back from reloading and reported in. Jerry Watson said, "Seven-Six, you see that yellow house with the tile roof next to that road?"

Norm in T-76 said, "Yeah, I've got it."

"I want you to drop your whole load right on that house."

"Roger that, inbound now."

76's wing dipped, and the nose dropped as he dove toward the ground. Damn, I admired those guys for their skill and courage.

I held my breath as I watched the fire reach the brush growing next to the house. Suddenly, the brush burst into flames.

At the same time, Norm arrived overhead with a huge red cloud of retardant billowing from the belly of Tanker 76.

The yard and the house were now painted bright red, but the flames were gone. The vegetation steamed. Norm had made the drop in the nick of time.

Many homes were saved that day, several times by direct drops right on them as flames licked at the eaves. Not a single home was lost.

I flew over Sonora for an hour and a half, but the tankers made three trips each, sometimes dropping a whole load and other times with single doors, allowing four drops for each load. They delivered a total of twenty-four tons of retardant. It was enough to bring the fire to a screeching halt so the ground crews who worked the rest of the day could bring it completely under control.

Our two tanker pilots and the loading crews were heroes. The next day, we were on the front page of the local paper. The big headline at the top said, "The Airmen Who Saved Our Homes."

A few days later the town held a "thank-you" ceremony at the Air Attack base. A big crowd showed up wanting to meet us. We were celebrities.

A pretty young reporter from the local newspaper interviewed Ranger Watson and me. She said, "I heard that you two had to do a belly landing."

I said, "Yeah, we had a hydraulic failure. The wheels wouldn't come down. We took it to Santa Rosa and bellied it in there. It was basically a routine gear-up landing."

Without smiling, Jerry shook his head and said, "It wasn't my routine."

She printed that line at the end of her article as if it were a punch line.

Norm Foster, the author, and Jim Eakin.

The editor of The Union Democrat newspaper must have been a novelist, judging from the way he wrote up the coverage of the event.

He was very eloquent. I'm including it here.

The Sierra Lookout

Last week brought a news story the staff of the Union Democrat is not likely to forget.

It wasn't the season's biggest story. In fact, it was all over within a few minutes and easily cleaned up journalistically in a few paragraphs.

But it may have been the easiest story the staff will ever cover and, in a frightening way, one of the most beautiful.

I speak of the fire that erupted last Tuesday in heavy, dry brush on the east edge of Sonora.

All reporters who had not left the building for lunch had a direct view of the fire, the deft attack on it and the quick victory over it without leaving their desks in the Democrat's second floor newsroom.

The Staff had just finished its work on Tuesday's paper and sent it on its way to the press when smoke was seen on the ridge, just beyond the silver dome of the old grammar school building.

The base of the fire, its exact location, could not be seen, but the anger and vigor of the smoke indicated that its source was not far beyond the ridge – and only a brush-covered leap from hillside homes east of Barretta St.

Tuesday was one of those summer days that flat landers seldom see. The air was hot and dry but without a hint of haze. Certainly, the air was not crisp, but it had enough edge to accent colors and sharpen definitions.

The setting and atmosphere were perfect for the colorful drama that took place.

First came easy white puffs, then angry bronze billows, as much flame as smoke, followed by intermittent surges of black, almost like explosions.

Reporters were still gathering their photographic equipment when the roar of the first attack plane was heard overhead.

The yellow bomber lifted a wing against the blue midday sky and dove toward the churning smoke.

When the snub-nosed plane reached the ridge, its path was low and level. There followed a moment of steady flight, then into the sunlit storm the plane disgorged its flame-snuffing wine, a massive splash of deep burgundy.

There was a furious snapping of camera shutters as reporters, now stretching out of the windows to their waists, tried to record the spectacular crescendo.

With black and white film, the effort was futile. They might just as well have tried to capture the New York philharmonic with a pocket tape recorder or use a flashbulb to catch the wonder of a starry night.

Although the fire attack scene may not have been recorded in all its color, it will surely remain vivid in the minds of all who watched, and its message will not soon be forgotten:

Whatever reordering of local priorities may take place, a strong attack force against fire deserves the highest rating.

HCM

***

Sometimes, on days off, I drove down to Modesto to hang out with my brothers from the Hangmen Motorcycle Club and pretend it was the distant past of 1969 instead of 1981.

There's a lot of open country around Sonora, and on some days off I'd be out hiking mountain trails, along rivers and creeks, or visiting some of the popular swimming holes in the area. At one lovely spot called Natural Bridges, you can swim through a cavern and come out on the other side of the mountain. The water was always freezing, even in the middle of summer, but it was a wonderful experience.

I hung out a lot with the Helitack crew, who were closer to my age than the tanker pilots. They were in their early twenties, while I was in my late twenties. Some evenings we'd go into town to hit the local bars for a few beers.

There was also a movie theater in town. In my first year there, I saw a memorable movie called *Raiders of the Lost Ark* with Harrison Ford. Finally, a movie that was just as exciting as my current lifestyle.

It was only four years before, in Alaska, that I had seen a fantastic movie called *Star Wars*, in which it seemed all the stars were pilots; Luke

Skywalker, Han Solo, and even Darth Vader (not exactly a hero) were pilots. I didn't realize it at the time, but looking back, I think it had a huge effect on me. Maybe if a guy like Darth Vader could be a pilot, I could too.

Now here I was hanging out in the foothills of the Sierra Nevada mountains, flying airplanes almost every day. It was my best summer vacation since I'd spent time in the county road camp nine years before.

Life is like riding a bicycle.
To keep your balance you must keep moving.
~Albert Einstein

Chapter 10
Looking for work again

Unfortunately, it had to end. By late September there were so few fires that they sent us home. It didn't pay much, but I was building flight time in the most exciting job I'd ever had. I would have done that all year if I could.

In the off-season, I was left to find whatever flying jobs I could. I had no desire to do any other kind of work.

I did some freelance instructing. One of my students rented a Piper Lance from Hemet-Ryan Aviation and hired me to fly him and four of his construction crew to Fresno, where they were doing a job for J.C. Penney. My logbook says it was IFR all the way to Fresno with an ILS approach to minimums. Given that I'd previously done construction, he paid me to work with his crew for five days. Then I flew us all back to Hemet.

Another part-time job was hauling skydivers, sometimes in Cessna 182s, Beech 18s, and the venerable old DC-3, flying as copilot with Howie Bohl. He later did a lot of movie work as a pilot flying old airplanes. After that he went to work at the commuter Imperial Airlines, then went on to United Airlines.

There were a few aircraft deliveries, and I even tried towing gliders. That might have been more productive if the instructor I flew with to get checked out hadn't been an old Marine Corps pilot. He seemed to think the way to teach pilots was by yelling and insulting them. In other words, he was a complete idiot.

After three flights I told him to go to hell and left, never to return. I didn't need any job that badly.

Fall turned into winter. The months seemed to drag by like a turtle that had no place important to be.

In late January 1982 Sis-Q Chief Pilot Harry Chaffee called me and wanted to know if I wanted to fly for him again.

He said, "I've still got your seat at Columbia this year if you want it."

The idea of getting back to life with my friends at the Air Attack base sounded wonderful, and I couldn't say "yes" fast enough. Then I ventured, "Do you have any tanker seats open?"

"No, sorry, we had an opening in Tanker 77, but I had to fill it with a guy who has years of experience."

I was a little disappointed but happy to have steady work again, even if it was for only four months.

Then Harry asked, "How are you doing otherwise? Are you working?"

"I'm getting some flight instructing in now and then. Pretty hard to pay the rent on that, though."

"Tell you what. If you'd like to come up here and work in the hangar, I'll give you a job until the fire season."

"That sounds good, but I'm not a mechanic, y'know."

"Don't worry about that. There are plenty of jobs around here where you can help out and that you don't need a license for."

I packed what few belongings I had in my old Pontiac and headed out for the nine-hour drive north. Using the want ads in a Santa Rosa newspaper, I found a one-room studio apartment for rent. The next morning I reported for work at Sis-Q.

The pay was just above minimum wage, but it beat working at McDonald's. I knew almost everyone working there and already had a reputation as "the guy who did a great job bellying in the O-2."

I just did what they told me, helping the mechanics work on airplanes. I was more of a gopher, and the work was easy. The pay was enough for my little apartment, gas in my car, and food on the table.

I also worked on the big DC-4 and DC-6 tankers – old airliners from the 1940s and 50s, now used as firefighting aircraft. When I had a chance, I sat in the cockpit and imagined what it would be like to be a copilot and, eventually, a captain in one of those big historic airplanes.

The weather was cold and often rainy but warm enough for lush green grass to grow everywhere that wasn't paved with asphalt.

The guys I worked with were friendly, accepting, and highly knowledgeable mechanics. Many became friends for years. Going out for dinner and beers got to be a regular thing. They were built-in buddies who came with the job. What a deal.

One Friday, in the lunchroom, one of the mechanics, named Dave, said, "Hey, guys, there's a nightclub over in Sebastopol that's having male strippers tonight!"

Everyone turned to stare at him, waiting for the punch line.

Neil Emory said, "Just because you like male strippers doesn't mean we do."

"No, man, you don't understand. No guys are allowed until nine o'clock. Then the dancers are done, and they open the doors to men. The place is full of half-drunk women having a good time. I'm telling you, it'll be fun."

The rest of us agreed to give it a try. So, at 8:30, we brave adventurers met at the J.C. Penney parking lot on Guerneville Road, and eight of us piled into two cars to carpool to Sebastopol.

We arrived at ground zero before nine to a full parking lot. It was impossible to find a spot, so we parked on the street.

Our little group walked to the entrance, where a few guys stood outside, waiting for the front door to open.

While waiting, we talked of other things: sports, airplanes, and TV shows like "Cheers," "Knight Rider," and "Remington Steele." We could hear the throbbing disco music and wild cheers, shouts, and applause from what sounded like a lot of women. From the looks of the parking lot, it was standing room only. Our imaginations ran wild. We exchanged nervous glances. I'm sure the others were thinking the same I was: "What are we getting ourselves into?"

Promptly at nine o'clock, the music stopped, the front door opened, and we cautiously walked into an unusual scene. The place was packed with happy, fun-loving women of all ages. It seemed everyone had a drink in their hand. The music started back up from a jukebox, not as loud this time.

Drinks were shoved into our hands: beer, wine, margaritas, or who knows what. Women took turns kissing us, giving us hugs, groping certain body parts, then moving on. It was nothing personal; we were guys and they were happy women. They were in the majority, and it was their bar.

The music played non-stop, and there was a dancefloor filled with women dancing with each other. Sometimes a few men were dragged out to dance whether they wanted to or not, usually with two or three women at a time.

We guys were being treated like objects, not individuals. I wasn't offended but intrigued, even fascinated, by the role reversal.

One woman in a crowd of fifty excited men would be anywhere from uncomfortable to terrified. Meanwhile, one man among fifty excited women would think he'd died and gone to heaven. There were a lot more than fifty women in this bar.

I felt like I understood their enthusiasm for the tables being turned, at least temporarily, and I thoroughly enjoyed their excitement and sense of freedom as they let it all hang out… so to speak.

Most of them probably had husbands or boyfriends waiting at home. Our small group of men was no threat to them, and nothing was expected of us.

I don't remember a single conversation. It was too noisy anyway and no one was there to talk.

After an hour our designated drivers were rounding us up, saying, "C'mon, we gotta go."

Thinking it was all over too soon, I followed our group out the door, glad for the respite. I almost felt like I'd been dragged into the Roman Colosseum to fight for my life – fortunately, without all the blood and death. I felt exhausted, but it had been exhilarating.

The ride back to Santa Rosa was full of laughter and funny stories about the adventures we'd had. I thought, 'The next time anyone wants to go back to that place, I'm in!'

***

After a month at Sis-Q, one of the mechanics asked me, "Hey, don't you have an instructor rating?"

I said, "Yeah. I'm also an instrument instructor. Why?

"I heard there's a little flight school up in Healdsburg that needs an instructor, if you're interested."

"Where's Healdsburg?"

"About twenty minutes north on the 101."

"I'll check it out. Thanks."

On my next day off I drove up to the airport in Healdsburg. I walked in and introduced myself, and they hired me immediately. As I've said, making a living as a flight instructor is difficult but working part-time on weekends was a good way to make a little extra money and get some flight time.

They had an old Cessna 150 and an even older Cherokee 140. I had plenty of experience in both. They were good training airplanes. Also, there was a beautiful red and black Cessna 177 Cardinal, numbered N54543. It was a sleek single-engine, retractable, four-seater. It was the kind of airplane I would have liked to own if I could have afforded it.

N54543

Students were already on a waiting list. All I had to do was schedule my time on the weekends. Nine o'clock at the male stripper bars would have to wait.

Between working at the Sis-Q hangar, hanging out with my new friends, and flight instructing on the weekends, wintertime flew by with a study job for a change. It was a nice time in my life.

I'd been instructing part-time at Healdsburg for three months. I learned our Helitack firefighter buddy, Art Chavira, was getting married in his hometown of Silver City, New Mexico.

Matt, who was in the Marine Reserves, was another close friend in the Helitack crew and a flight student of mine. He asked if there was any way some of us could fly down there to attend the wedding.

At first I said no, but then I got to thinking: If I got the others to chip in, we could rent the Cessna Cardinal from the flight school as a private charter. The flight school would get some paid time on the airplane and we could fly down there to attend the wedding.

On Thursday I took a couple of days off from my job at the hangar and drove to Healdsburg airport. No one was there when I got the keys to the Cardinal and blocked it off the schedule for the next four days. I expected us to be back on Sunday.

Margaret was one of the Columbia Helitack firefighters who showed up for the trip. She didn't look like a typical firefighter. She was more like one of Hemingway's granddaughters – a beautiful face and a very fit body. I think some of the firefighters and pilots might have been a bit in love with her.

However, she didn't seem to know any of that. She just wanted to be "one of the guys," a firefighter, and she worked as hard as the rest of them.

We flew in the Cardinal to the Santa Maria airport just south of San Luis Obispo and north of Vandenberg Air Force Base, where we picked up Matt. I let him do most of the flying and navigating. It was a great opportunity for him to get some cross-country experience. We flew to Phoenix's Deer Valley Airport to pick up Matt's cousin Chuck, who would later become a CH-53 helicopter pilot and a high-ranking officer in the Marine Corps.

As we progressed southeast into the dark and stormy night, thunderstorms blocked our path. We dodged this way and that. It was getting late when I decided to divert to Wilcox, Arizona, where we could spend the night after eight hours of flying. After calling a taxi, we got rooms at a cheap motel. In the morning we landed in Silver City in time for Art's wedding.

A funny thing happened while we were in the church. Just before the ceremony, we were all duded up in our best clothes. I wore my best and only leisure suit. Suddenly Matt turned to me with a concerned look on his face and, in a tense voice, said, "Do you have a knife?"

As I regressed to my former life, my first thought was that there was trouble with someone. Lifting my pant leg, I snatched the double-bladed Gerber commando dagger from its scabbard strapped to my ankle and handed it to him.

The people near us audibly gasped when they saw the weapon being produced in a church, at a wedding.

Matt's eyes widened as he took the blade. It turned out the "emergency" he needed it for was an errant thread on the bride's wedding gown.

Expertly eliminating the threatening thread, he handed the knife back. I sheepishly returned it to the ankle sheath while mumbling an apology to those nearby.

We partied it up the rest of the day and night, celebrating their wedding. Probably because of the knife incident, most of the guests gave me a wide berth, avoiding eye contact. They didn't seem to want to talk to me. It wasn't bad enough that I was a gringo – worse, I was a dangerous gringo.

The next morning, all too early because of a slight hangover, we were back in the air retracing our route to the West Coast.

Cessna 177RG Cardinal

Once again, we dodged thunderstorms, only this time it was during the day when we could see them better. After landing in Phoenix again, we dropped off Chuck, then continued our flight into California. We spent the night in Santa Maria at Matt's parents' house.

The next day, it was beautiful weather, with blue skies: "clear and a million," as pilots like to say. Margaret and I flew northward, enjoying the scenery with the California coastline below us and the endless deep blue of the Pacific Ocean to our left as far as we could see.

The weather was still perfect when we landed at Healdsburg on May 3. It was Monday, and we'd been gone five days, longer than planned. Margaret grabbed her small bag and, after a quick hug, headed to her car.

I walked to the small office of the flight school to drop off the keys to the airplane. The owner of the flight school was there.

He was a little upset with me. "What the hell do you think you're doing taking my airplane without my permission?"

I said, "I was doing a charter flight. The Cardinal is part of the fleet, is it not? I'd blocked it out until Sunday, but we got delayed coming back due to weather."

Handing him the keys, I pulled out enough cash to pay for the seventeen-plus hours I'd put on the plane.

After he got the money he said, "You're fired!"

Oops!

I shrugged and said, "I thought you'd be happy to get paid for a long charter flight like that."

He said, "I was planning on going somewhere this weekend."

I said, "You're right. I should have checked with you. My apologies."

I was embarrassed about getting fired, but I didn't really need the job any longer. I had only two more weeks to work at the Sis-Q hangar before I was scheduled to be back in Columbia to start my second season as the Air Attack pilot there. The memorable trip to Silver City with my friends had been worth it, and we'd paid full price for the rental of the Cardinal.

Soon I was saying goodbye, for now, to the friends I'd been working with in Santa Rosa.

I moved out of my one-room studio apartment, threw my two bags in my car, and drove east to the foothills of the Sierras.

Another brief segment of my life was over as I headed toward more adventure. My aviation career was moving forward, and that was all that mattered.

An early morning at Sis-Q Flying Service

Fear of danger is ten thousand times more terrifying than danger itself.

~ Unknown

Chapter 11
Back into the fire

Back at Columbia for the 1982 fire season, Norm and I rented the same single-wide mobile home, space 13, in the RV park next to the airport. This year was a bit different, as our buddy Jim Eakin was now stationed in Hollister, flying Tanker 96.

A new guy was driving Tanker 77. His name was Jerry Donahue. We called him JD.

He was friendly and relaxed, with dark eyes and an easy smile that gleamed from his black beard. He was thin and wiry, quiet and unassuming, with a mop of dark hair over his forehead. He wasn't new to aerial firefighting. Having started in 1975, he'd been flying numerous aircraft, including a World War II-era B-17 for years.

The company for which he'd worked had retired that airplane. It was probably worth too much money to use as a tanker because so few of them were left. So, he'd gotten a job with Sis-Q manning the office of Tanker 77. It would be his first season in a single-seat tanker. He was a great guy and a good pilot. We almost died together.

Tanker pilots are a fascinating group of people. It takes a special person to do that job.

Bob Valet, another tanker pilot from Sis-Q, showed up in a twin-engine Cessna 402 to take us to Santa Rosa, where we'd pick up our airplanes. Jim Aiken was already on board. It was good to see him again.

When we got to the Sonoma base, Bob gave me my training ride to make sure I hadn't forgotten how to fly the O-2. It was a good chance to practice with an engine out and doing map drops. All the pilots went through the same routine, except that tanker pilots also made water drops.

After the training flight, I test-flew 440 and found that the directional gyro (an electronic compass) didn't work. When I got back, I notified the mechanics. Because I was done flying for the day, I walked around the hangar visiting some of the guys I'd worked with. That evening Jim and I went out for Thai food and Japanese beer. We invited Norm to join us. He wrinkled his nose and said, "I don't eat that kind of food."

The next day I did a quick check ride with Blaine Moore, the battalion chief. With the new directional gyro installed, I ferried 440 back to Columbia, ready for business.

When we arrived at our first fire of the 1982 season, the tankers were already on station and in their left-hand orbits at one thousand feet over the fire. Jerry Watson and I arrived and pulled into our standard right-hand orbit at fifteen hundred feet.

Quickly sizing up the scene, Ranger Watson said, "Okay, Seven-Six, I want you to put all four doors in trail at the head of the fire, starting at that dirt road."

Norm said, "You got it."

Fifteen hundred feet below, we watched Norm's airplane almost merge with its shadow on the ground as the doors opened one at a time and he painted a long red line in front of the fire as if his S-2 was a huge spray can.

As we orbited, I breathed in that now-familiar smell of woodland fire smoke. It was exhilarating to fire pilots because it brought action and danger. However, it was terrifying to people who lived on the ground because it destroyed homes and lives.

Also, there were the colors that had so vividly painted my memories of the previous season: the yellow and red flames, the dry grass, the green trees, the crimson retardant, and the black of the burned areas. It would have been beautiful if it hadn't been so devastating to people and animals caught in its path.

I was happy to be back on the job.

Jerry continued on the radio: "Seven-Seven, I want you to do the same thing, starting where he leaves off."

JD said, "Roger."

As soon as Norm made his drops, he pointed his airplane back to base to reload in case he was needed back at the fire. It was standard procedure.

Out the right-hand window, we saw Tanker 77 swoop down and put a line of retardant to continue what 76 had done.

Watching him climb back up off the fire, Jerry turned to me and said, "Take us down for a closer look."

Pulling back the throttles, I started a descent to one thousand feet as we circled right.

Leveling off, I added some power. As my eyes left the altimeter to the RPM and manifold pressure gauges, I turned to look out the right window to make sure we were over the spot Jerry wanted to see.

We were both looking out the window when Tanker 77 suddenly filled the window, flashing past in the opposite direction. There had to be mere feet between our wingtips.

The S-2 looked enormous at that close range, and it was gone as quickly as it had appeared.

Jerry's head snapped around as he looked at me with an expression of complete shock. It was so fast his headset slid around his face so that the left earpiece was now sitting over his nose and between his wide eyes. My eyes were probably just as big.

Shoving in the throttles, I leveled the wings while pulling the nose up and started a climb away from the tanker's altitude.

Almost in a daze, Watson said, "I thought he went back to base."

Still in shock, I said, "So did I."

Jerry slowly straightened his headset back over his ears and took some deep breaths. Trying to control his anger, he keyed the mike and said, "Seven-Seven, why didn't you return to base?"

JD came back, "I've still got two doors left."

"I told you to drop all four."

"You did? Oh, sorry."

Sitting on the left side of his aircraft and looking down at the fire, JD hadn't seen us and didn't know how close he'd just come to dying.

Jerry calmly and deliberately said, "Tie your last two doors on that line and return to base."

Tanker 77 complied. This time, after the drop, Ranger Watson and I watched him climb out toward Columbia.

Unfortunately, mid-air collisions have happened too often during aerial firefighting operations. This little miscommunication had very nearly cost three people their lives.

Ranger Watson and I sat in stunned silence. Being a consummate professional, he wasn't going to let his feelings out while on the job.

He didn't seem to blame me. We'd both assumed Tanker 77 had left the area to return to base.

I hadn't been watching for other air traffic as well as I should have been. This violated one of the most basic rules of airmanship: "See and avoid." I'd let my situational awareness slip and I felt terrible about it. We got lucky, but I vowed not to let it happen again.

*The greatest danger for most of us is not that we aim too high
and miss it, but that it is too low and we reach it.*

~ Michelangelo

Chapter 12
Ted Bell

Ted Bell leaned forward and squinted through the smoke outside the windscreen of the big DC-6 air tanker. The four big radial engines were roaring after coming off a drop on a fire in the high country a little north and west of Healdsburg, California. A ridgeline was somewhere out there. Glancing at the altimeter, he knew they had to climb another couple of hundred feet to clear it.

He was in the copilot's seat. To his left, in what seemed more like a small room than a cockpit, was Gary, the captain. He was flying the airplane, as he always did when dispersing retardant. They were both straining to see where they were going because the smoke had gotten thicker than it had been on the last drop.

Gary was a hero in the air tanker business: tall, with Hollywood good looks, blond hair, and an athletic build. He was a very good pilot and a bit of a daredevil. A favorite pastime when he wasn't flying was riding his Harley.

Ted was also tall and slender, with a sweeping mustache that would have looked more at home under a cowboy hat while on a horse. He wasn't new to the aerial firefighting business, having already flown for several years as an Air Attack pilot. This was his first season in an air tanker.

The four Pratt and Whitney R-2800 Double Wasp engines were each putting out twenty-four hundred horsepower. The airplane was climbing well after dropping its load of two thousand gallons of Phos-Chek retardant.

Ted glanced nervously at the manifold pressure gauges, the prop RPMs, and the cylinder head temperatures to make sure nothing was going over the redline.

Then he yelled to Gary over the roar of the four motors: "I think that'll do it for the day. That fire is almost out."

Gary replied, "I hope not. I can use all the flight pay I can get."

Tanker pilots get paid for their time in the air. You don't make money sitting on the ground. A long time ago, an air tanker pilot had been arrested for starting fires so he could get more flight time. Tanker pilots tended to joke about things like that all the time.

Just then the Air Attack called them and said, "Tanker Two One, load and return."

Gary looked at Ted and smiled.

They were still accelerating to their climb speed when Gary reached down to the right, at the back of the center pedestal, to bring the flaps up. For that couple of seconds, he wasn't watching where they were going.

Ted was annoyed. As copilot, that was his job. Whoever was flying was supposed to be looking out the window or locked onto the instruments if you were in clouds – or, in this case, smoke. He glanced left as Gary flew like he was the only one in the cockpit but then forced himself to look outside.

Once again, he glanced at the altimeter. It looked like they'd clear the ridge. Directing his attention back outside, he froze with a shock of adrenaline. As if in a nightmare, Ted saw an obstruction rushing at them out of the smoke.

He yelled, "TREE!", but it was too late. Just clearing the ridgeline, they plowed into the tall pine tree, taking the impact on the left side of the aircraft's nose. Ted instinctively ducked forward behind the instrument panel and closed his eyes.

The impact was "like a bomb going off." The windshield in front of Gary exploded with plexiglass and wood chips, and a sudden hurricane of wind and noise blasted into the normally controlled atmosphere of the cockpit. Ted sat up and looked left. He saw Gary with bloody hands over his eyes and realized he was in no condition to fly.

A branch about five feet long and "as thick as your arm" had come through the windscreen like a crude spear, embedding itself into the bulkhead behind Gary's seat.

If he hadn't been leaning over to bring up the flaps, he'd have been killed. But then, if he hadn't been operating the flaps and had been watching where he was going, they might not have hit the tree.

The noise was deafening as debris swirled through the cockpit and the airplane shuddered and shook. Gary couldn't see anything because of wood chips, and probably glass, in his eyes.

The airplane buffeted on the edge of a stall. They were about to crash! Ted grabbed the controls, pushed the nose down, and instinctively shoved the four throttles even farther forward.

They had just crossed the ridge, and luckily the terrain now dropped away. That was the only thing saving them. They needed to go downhill to pick up speed, and now nothing was in their way.

Even with the nose down and the throttles at full power, the DC-6 wasn't accelerating as it should. The shaking from the stall buffet had subsided, but a faster vibration had taken its place. Absent-mindedly, Ted thought, 'Bent propellers.'

Daring to take his eyes off the terrain as they sailed down the backside of the ridge, Ted checked the engine instruments. He found that the number two engine had quit and the other three were overheating like crazy. Number three, the inboard engine on the right, was the worst. Instinctively, he pulled back the number two throttle, hoping the auto-feather system would work, but he didn't have time to verify it. From the cockpit, he couldn't see if that propeller was turned into the windstream. He rolled in some right rudder trim to compensate for the dead engine.

Wood debris and pine boughs from the tree were likely packed into the front of the engine cowls, preventing the airflow necessary to keep the cylinders and oil cool. He opened all the cowl flaps, but it seemed to do no good. It served only to slow the airplane a little more.

Easing back the power to keep the engines from burning up, he kept the nose pointed down and wondered how long that could continue before they hit the ground. If he let the airspeed deteriorate to where the wing stalled, he'd be screwed. If he let the engines get so hot that they quit, he'd be screwed.

Into his boom microphone, he called the Sonoma Air Attack Base: "Sonoma, Tanker Two One, Mayday!"

"Tanker Two One, what's your emergency?"

"We had a tree strike, the captain is incapacitated, the aircraft won't hold altitude, one engine is out, and the others are overheating. I'm not sure if we can make the runway."

After a brief pause, Sonoma base came back on the radio and said, "Tanker Two One, Santa Rosa Tower says you're cleared to land on any runway. The airport is yours. They're rolling the emergency equipment."

A mini tornado of wind in the cockpit blew wood splinters, broken glass, and pieces of bark around. The debris pelted them as Ted squinted and tried to protect his eyes so he could fly. He had to yell into the microphone over the noise: "Roger that, Sonoma, we'll do the best we can."

He glanced at Gary, who still held his hands over his face and was now huddled forward under the instrument panel, trying to stay out of the gale of air blasting through the smashed windshield.

Ted experimented with pushing the throttles up and watching the temperature gauges. They kept losing altitude and couldn't gain air speed to give a comfortable margin for anything resembling normal flight.

Glancing through the windshield, he was encouraged when he saw the Santa Rosa airport in the distance but discouraged at the constant loss of altitude. This airplane didn't want to stay in the air.

When he pushed the throttles up, the cylinder head temperatures went into the red line and the vertical speed indicator, or VSI, fluctuated between descent rates of three hundred and five hundred feet per minute. When he pulled them back, the airspeed slowed toward a stall.

Ted felt a chill go down his spine as he realized this might be it. On his left, he could see Highway 101, which he knew paralleled runway 14. He turned southeast with the highway to his left and kept nursing the stricken aircraft toward the airport.

Then a horrible thought hit him. What if they crashed short of the runway in a residential area, a business district, or, worse yet: a school?

Nothing in the world could be worse than crashing into a school. Before becoming a tanker pilot, Ted had been a high school teacher.

However, he'd been so enamored with the whole aerial firefighter idea that he'd resigned from his job with the school district and begun flying lessons. It had been a long road, and now here he was, in charge of a crippled air tanker, with lives in the balance. A thought flashed through his mind: "Maybe I should have stayed in the classroom."

He started thinking he shouldn't be trying to save himself and Gary. Maybe he should just put this thing on the ground in an open field before other people got hurt or killed. That would be unacceptable.

Glancing nervously at the altimeter and VSI, he tried to do the math in his head: altitude, distance, descent rate, time. They were down to three thousand feet and still dropping. Ted could see the thin, dark ribbon of the runway in the distance.

In his headset, he heard Sonoma base say, "Tanker Two One, contact Santa Rosa Tower on one-one-eight-point-one. Good luck."

He acknowledged, "Thanks," and switched the comm one radio. "Santa Rosa Tower, Tanker Two One, emergency aircraft inbound."

"Tanker Two One, we have you at eight miles northwest, cleared to land on One Four, emergency equipment standing by."

"Roger, Santa Rosa, thanks."

ATC asked their required questions for an emergency aircraft: "Tanker Two One, say souls on board and fuel in minutes."

Glancing over at Gary to see if he was still alive, Ted said, "Uh… Two souls on board I think, fuel… I have no idea, more than we need."

"Roger that, Two One, cleared to land on One Four."

"Cleared to land. We're going to need an ambulance for the captain."

The tower said, "They're standing by."

Ted felt his palms sweating as he gripped the yoke and struggled with the crippled air tanker. It wallowed through the air toward their salvation: a beautiful, long, straight blacktopped runway stretching out ahead of them.

He was worried about putting the gear down, knowing it would slow the airplane, which was already too slow.

He saw residential areas with houses between him and the airport.

He decided those arbitrary marks on the engine gauges were there for normal situations. This was anything but normal.

With his left hand on the three operating throttles, he eased them forward until the temperatures went past the redline on the gauges. He thought, 'Either these engines are going to blow up or we're going to crash. Right now, it doesn't make much difference.'

He glanced from the runway to the instrument panel. Ted was encouraged when the airplane started to hold level flight for the first time in ten minutes. The vibration increased. How long would the engines last? If necessary, he'd destroy the engines to make it to the runway.

Chief Pilot Harry Chaffee had been listening to the radio in the Air Attack office. He walked quickly to the edge of the runway to watch. Word had gotten around, so most of the mechanics of Sis-Q Flying Service filtered out. They were on pins and needles as they saw the wounded DC-6 coming in while pulling a thin trail of smoke. They weren't just coworkers; they were friends. Everyone held their breath, and probably a few prayers were being said.

Someone pointed and shouted, "There they are!"

Somebody else said, "Man, they're really low."

Ted watched the dark strip of asphalt slowly widen as they neared the runway. One at a time, he wiped his sweaty palms on his pant legs. He knew he had to have the runway made before he put the gear down. They'd get only one chance at this.

Nervously eyeing the oil and cylinder head temperatures, which were past the redline, he eased the throttles back to start a descent toward the runway. The temperatures of engines one and four came down a bit, though number three's did not.

Now on a glidepath toward the rapidly approaching runway, he knew they'd make it as long as the airplane didn't stall when he put the gear down. Risking more drag, he put down only the first notch of flaps to increase lift over the wings.

Finally crossing the threshold of runway 14, without looking, Ted reached down to his left at the back of the control pedestal, grabbed the gear handle, and shoved it to the down position. He held his breath while easing the throttles back, then rolled in some nose-up trim on the wheel by his left knee. He thought, 'If the gear doesn't make it down, this is going to get really noisy.'

Keeping the airspeed indicator just above stall speed, they sank toward the runway. They were landing whether the wheels got all the way down or not.

Just as he was bringing the nose up in a flair, the three green lights lit up on the instrument panel in front of him. He let out a big sigh as the four main wheels chirped onto the runway. Then he pulled the throttles back to idle as the nose wheel came down. The big airplane slowed even before he applied the brakes. Using the rudder pedals, he kept it on the centerline until he came to a stop right next to the fire engines and ambulance sitting on the edge of the asphalt.

Ted shut down the engines, which quietly clicked as they slowed to a stop. In the sudden eerie silence, he saw his friends on the side of the runway, jumping up and down and cheering. Ted looked over at Gary and, almost incredulously, said, "We made it."

Gary finally sat up, took his hands away from his face, and said, "Are my eyes still there?"

"Yeah, I think you're going to be okay."

Gary said, "Thanks, man, nice job!"

Tanker 21 at Santa Rosa before the tree strike.

No, I wasn't there, but Ted told me this story about three months after it happened, while I was working at Sis-Q in Santa Rosa during the off-season.

Two years later, in 1984, Ted was flying out of Ukiah on a fast-moving fire near Clear Lake. A ground crew of firefighters was in trouble and about to get overrun by the fire. It is believed Ted tried to take a shortcut up a canyon and over a ridge to get to the firefighters who were in danger.

He was reluctant to drop his load of retardant until the last minute, which would have improved the airplane's performance. Ted's S-2 hit the mountain one hundred and fifty feet below the ridgeline. He was the first tanker pilot to die that year.

In 1998, after a long career, Gary also crashed and died while working on a fire in an S-2.

I relate this story to pay tribute to the bravery and skill of the tanker pilots and to show how dangerous their jobs are.

I always wanted to be one of them, but Chief Pilot Harry Chaffee never wanted to put me in a tanker. He told me more than once, "This is no business for a young guy like you. You should get yourself a real job."

It always annoyed me, but after hearing that Ed Real, one of the most experienced tanker pilots, crashed in 1984, I realized all my bravado and overconfidence wouldn't overcome the realities of the danger of this business. Harry probably saved my life.

Danger is very real; fear is a choice.
~Will Smith

Chapter 13

Why did I want to do this again?

Unless pilots live in Kansas and expect to never fly outside Kansas, they need to learn about "mountain flying."

Winds and currents act entirely differently in the mountains than they do in lower elevations or the flatlands – not to mention density altitude.

If you fly a lot in the mountains, it's easy to start thinking the wind and the terrain are out to get you.

As with politics or warfare, you must understand the game in order to survive. As the FAA says in one of its PDFs, "Mountain flying has a narrow window of safety."

Sometimes we were operating on fires in the lowlands of the San Joaquin Valley. They were usually fast-moving, wind-driven grassfires for which mountain flying wasn't an issue.

More often we were in the foothills of the Sierra Nevada mountains. The higher the altitude, the more dangerous it got.

For the guys flying the tankers, it was even worse. They had to get down low and very close to the fires and to the ground. The United States has a lot of mountains and, in the west, very big mountains! California has more than its share.

Downdrafts and updrafts are obvious, but you also have to learn about wind shear, mountain waves, and rotor winds. Most of the time they're invisible unless there are clouds or smoke.

The last thing you want to do is get on the backside of a mountain where the air is flowing downward. It's like flying into an invisible waterfall, and it can drive you right into the ground.

In my old job as a flight instructor/charter pilot, I was bringing some passengers back to Hemet from Los Angeles International Airport. We were flying eastbound over Saddleback Mountain on the east side of Orange County. The air was smooth as we crossed the ridge with about five hundred feet to spare. This was no problem, as the wind was at our backs. However, after crossing the ridge, we hit moderate turbulence and the small plane seemed to fall out of the sky.

It was like we were riding that waterfall I mentioned. We were in a mountain wave and lost about one thousand feet in altitude. My passengers turned white. Later, they said they thought they were going to die.

I stayed calm because thousands of feet were still below us now that we were past the ridgeline of the mountain. We had somewhere to go, an escape route. However, if we'd encountered that downdraft in the opposite direction, the story would have been very different.

Late one afternoon, Captain Bob Sutton and I got a call to look for smoke up around Mi-Wuk Village, about twenty miles from Columbia. At four thousand six hundred feet above sea level, the town was quite a bit higher in altitude than Columbia. Density altitude started raising its ugly head and becoming a player.

Arriving over the town at fifty-five hundred feet above sea level, we were less than one thousand feet above the ground. We cruised around looking for signs of smoke. We looked down into the evening dusk as tall pine trees reached toward the airplane.

Mi-Wuk is a nice small town on Highway 108, which heads into the high Sierras and over the top, then down into the Owens Valley. It's a terrific ride on a motorcycle in the summertime but a little cold in the winter.

Bob wasn't seeing anything, so he asked me to take us down lower to get a better look at what he thought was smoke. When we got to it, we saw campers standing around the fire. They waved to us as we passed overhead, almost on the treetops.

I was enjoying zooming around at a low level while trying to spot that pesky wisp of smoke that someone had reported.

Bob would tell me, "Turn this way, turn that way." I complied and was increasingly losing my sense of situational awareness.

Looking down through the trees, we saw scattered homes in a loose-knit neighborhood, some having barbeques and family gatherings.

It looked like a great place to live. My mind wandered, "What would it be like to live down there?" I had no permanent address, and my only home at the moment was the rented single-wide trailer near the airport that I shared with Norm. I was an itinerant pilot moving to where the jobs took me.

I absent-mindedly wondered what it would be like to have a permanent home in a pleasant little place like this. I was getting distracted.

Remembering my pilot duties, I glanced through the windshield and noticed a ridge ahead of us. It got my attention because I was looking up at it. Sliding the throttles forward, I checked the manifold pressure gauges and trimmed the nose up for a climb.

The nose came up, but the airspeed started dropping. I pushed the throttles up more until they were at maximum. Then I pushed the prop levers up to where they, too, were at max.

I pulled the nose up to stay above the trees. The airspeed was still falling, and I realized too late that we were in a pickle. I looked to my right at Bob to see if he was aware of what was going on. He was still focusing out the right window, looking for smoke.

We were at the bottom of a shallow canyon that went uphill on both sides and uphill in front of us. The airspeed had dropped so low that I was afraid to bank left or right to try a U-turn. Banking too far at low speed would increase the stall speed, and we were so low the wingtip might hit the trees. We were trapped in the old "flying up a canyon" scenario. Never fly up a canyon! (Unless you're Tom Cruise in an F-18.)

I'd gotten us into this by not paying attention to my flying and by looking for smoke instead.

Not being a pilot, Bob didn't seem to notice the increasing engine power and pitch of the airplane. He was still calmly focusing out his side window, probably enjoying this little evening cruise over the thickly forested highlands.

With full power on both engines, I started sweating as I watched the airspeed get lower. I couldn't turn left or right, and the airplane was doing its best to climb, but it wasn't enough. The ridgeline ahead was coming closer, and it was still above us.

I thought about the stall speed number and wondered exactly what it would be at this altitude and weight. How slow could I get before we crashed into the top of the trees? Then, how far was it to the ground after that happened? They were very tall trees.

The airspeed dropped below the point where I thought the wing would stop flying. What little climb rate we had went to zero, then fell below it. Trying to lower the stall speed, I risked more drag by putting down the first notch of flaps, which would increase the lift a bit.

'This is it,' I thought. We'd plow into the tops of the trees, then plummet to the ground, and it would all be over. Just then the stall warning horn went off and, at the same time, we cleared the ridge. A valley was ahead of us. Feeling like the firing squad had just been told to stand down, I pushed the nose down into the valley and we started picking up speed.

The engines were still at full power, so we accelerated quickly. I pulled up the notch of flaps, not believing how lucky we'd been. I was rolling the trim wheel forward as Bob turned to me and asked, "What was that?"

Although my throat was bone dry, I managed to casually say, "Oh, just the, uh… stall warning horn. We got a little slow clearing that ridgeline."

He nodded knowingly and turned back to look out his side window. He didn't seem to notice how much I was sweating!

***

Not long into the '82 fire season, we were working a big fire near a small town called Chinese Camp. Because of the gold rush, they have a lot of "Camps" in California. French Camp, Angels Camp, Fish Camp… It's a long list.

It was July 27 and they called it the Firestone Fire. Soon the fire got big enough that they started calling in help from other bases: Buzz

Blaylock and Roger Stark from Grass Valley, Ed Real in Tanker 100 from Hollister, and my buddy Jim Eakin in Tanker 96, to name a few.

I'd just seen Jim a month ago at Santa Rosa as we were getting checked out again and picking up our airplanes. One evening we had a chance to go out for dinner and a couple of beers.

When he arrived at the scene, I said hi on the discrete pilot-to-pilot frequency. We chatted briefly while he waited for his turn to make his drop.

Ranger Watson and I had been flying on this fire for about four hours when he called in for a relief Air Attack to give us a break so we could refuel the airplane and get a bite to eat.

We hadn't been on the ground long when, while sitting in the kitchen area of the ready room of the Quonset hut making a ham sandwich, I heard those dreaded words over the loudspeaker system: "Tanker 96 has gone down."

I froze and felt a chill as my mouth dropped open, but no words came out. Suddenly lunch didn't sound very good. I looked over at Jerry Watson. He stared back expressionless for a couple of seconds, then looked down at the floor and slowly shook his head.

I felt lightheaded and short of breath, so I forced myself to inhale. I hoped beyond hope that Jim might have survived, but it wasn't to be. I don't think tanker pilots ever survive crashes on fires.

Flying into the low visibility of the smoke to make his drop, he hit a tree on the pull out, which took off the horizontal stabilizer on one side of his tail. Unable to pull the nose up, he crashed into a hillside. The airplane exploded on impact.

The aerial firefighting business is dangerous and has claimed a lot of lives over the years. I was only seasonal and had no intention of making a career of it, but in the early '80s, flying jobs were still hard to come by.

One of the greatest discoveries a person makes is to find they can do what they were frightened to do.

~ Henry Ford

Chapter 14
Don Ornbaum

Tanker pilot legend Don Ornbaum

Matt panted and sweated inside his yellow Nomex coveralls as he swung his Pulaski at the scrub oak and manzanita, struggling to keep his balance on the side of the steep river canyon. Working around him were six other firefighters from Columbia Helitack – highly experienced and very fit young firefighters. They were a small but elite crew.

Captain Gene Strand alternated between shouting instructions and talking on the radio to the ground boss and the airborne Air Attack, which today was Jerry Watson and me.

They were cutting a line to stop the approaching flames in a deep and narrow river canyon, on a fire being called Temperate Flat, north and east of the city of Fresno. It was a big fire, mostly grass and brush. Our Helitack crew was stationed on a small part of it.

Ranger Watson had sent them into the canyon with their instructions: "See if you can knock down those spot fires and keep the fire from crossing the river. If it gets on the other side, it's going to take off and head straight for that small town."

Working feverishly, soaked in sweat and covered with dirt, they'd been there for over an hour, having been literally dropped off by the big Bell UH-1F "Huey" helicopter. The hillside was so steep, they had to hang from the skid on the uphill side and drop to the ground. After the crew was off, the pilot deployed his bucket and started making water drops onto the flames.

The wind was picking up and the fire on the flat ground above the canyon was heading straight for their location. Embers carried by the wind were floating down all around them. Now, instead of just cutting a fire break, they were running from place to place, trying to put out numerous spot fires starting behind their position. Their best efforts were not enough, as too many new fires were popping up. As soon as they knocked down one fire, five more took its place.

They'd long since used up the contents of their back pumps, which were five-gallon tin water tanks worn on their backs with hoses to squirt the water onto the fires. The pumps were for little spot fires but useless in a raging brush fire. They weren't close enough to the river to refill them.

Gene felt the hot wind smack him on the opposite side of his face while the smoke thickened. He heard some of his firefighters shouting, "Wind change, wind change!"

With the fierce wind now howling up the canyon, the dry brush was exploding all around them. They realized they were trapped on the steep grade between the sheer rock face of a vertical escarpment above them and the San Joaquin River below.

The river had been their fallback position in case they got in trouble, but now a solid wall of flames was cutting off that pathway. Smoke enveloped them, and the spot fires that kept landing behind them had grown into another wall, surrounding them.

Captain Strand's voice sounded weak and far away in my earphones. I felt helpless as I listened. "Air Attack Four Four Zero, Helitack is in trouble down here. The wind has switched on us and we're running out of options. Can we get the helo back in here to pick us up?"

In his usual calm drawl, Ranger Watson said, "Helicopter Four Oh Four is refueling in Fresno. He'll be at least another twenty minutes."

Gene said, "We don't have twenty minutes!"

Looking into the faces of his fellow firefighters, he was met with blank stares and wide eyes. Heads were turning in all directions as if looking for a way out, but there was none. Matt yelled to Captain Strand, "Boss, this isn't looking good. We gotta get out of here!"

Gene hollered back, "I'm working on it. Pull everyone back to the center of this clearing and get ready to deploy."

Despite the blazing heat, Gene Strand felt a chill go down his spine as he realized they were trapped and in danger of being overrun. The radio traffic seemed to crackle with tension like static electricity. Struggling to keep his voice reasonably calm, Gene said, "Four Four

Zero, our escape route to the river has been cut off and we've got fire all around us. I'm requesting an emergency drop on our location."

Ranger Watson laconically replied, "Roger that, Helitack, I'll see what I can do."

Just then, while scanning for traffic against a backdrop of blue sky and brown smoke, I picked up two big red and white four-engine airplanes gracefully sailing inbound to our location.

They were the "heavies" and each carried three thousand gallons of Phos-Chek retardant.

The cavalry had arrived!

A deep voice came on the air-to-air frequency: "Four Four Zero, Tanker Six One is on scene."

This was followed by another voice: "Six Zero on scene."

Jerry said, "Good to see you guys. Tanker Six One, the Helitack crew is down in the river canyon and about to get overrun. I don't have any S2s available. Do you think you can get into that canyon and help them out?"

Tanker Six One responded, "Man, that's awfully tight in there. I see them just inside of that black smoke. It doesn't look good. I'll see what I can do."

The heavies were DC-7 airliners from the 1950s, with four huge eighteen-cylinder supercharged engines, each producing three thousand two hundred and fifty horsepower. Tanker Six One was first in line. Perhaps more importantly, its captain was none other than the legendary Don Ornbaum. He was known as the best tanker pilot in the business, and he could fly that big DC-7 like it were a jet fighter.

Captain Strand yelled at his crew to fall back and get ready to deploy their fire shelters. Smoke was stinging their eyes behind their goggles, and they were choking for air behind the bandanas over their faces. All around them were heat and smoke and flames, but straight up they could see blue sky.

Through my headphones, I heard Don say, "Air Attack, I don't want to try to go down that river. It's too narrow and I can't get close enough to the fire because of that canyon wall. I'm going to go in at ninety degrees."

"Okay, your call, Six One. You're cleared in."

"Just make sure those damn helicopters stay out of my way."

Jerry said, "No problem, they're all clear."

Then, to Helitack on the other frequency, "Get your heads down. There's a drop coming in."

While we orbited to the right at fifteen hundred feet over the fire, I watched out the right window as Tanker Six One dropped over the flat ground, its shadow racing to catch up with the airplane and seeming like it was losing.

The gear came down, then the flaps went to full. It appeared to slow. I was amazed when the tail kicked up and that big DC-7 disappeared as it dived straight down over the edge of the cliff.

A thought went through my mind: 'That's not possible.' A sense of dread flooded me. Just a week before, my friend Jim Eakin had crashed in the Keystone fire.

Captain Strand screamed to his crew, "We've got a tanker coming in. HIT THE DECK!"

Matt, instead of burying his face in the dirt, couldn't help but look up through the smoke toward the brown vertical cliff and the blue sky beyond. Expecting to see a smaller S-2, he was shocked by what appeared.

Two things stood out. The first was the size of the airplane. The second was the number "61" on the tail. He knew who was flying and was at once filled with hope and dread – hope because he knew of

Ornbaum's reputation as being the best and dread because he also knew of Ornbaum's reputation as being a little crazy.

Tanker 61.

With full flaps and landing gear down, the airplane looked like an enormous bird of prey, wings stretched out and talons reaching toward them. It got bigger every second as it came straight down at them. When it pitched over the edge of the cliff, Matt was amazed that he could see the top of the DC-7. He thought, 'There's no way he can pull out of that dive.'

The four huge propellers, each with four blades, looked like sixteen giant meat cleavers.

Then a cloud of crimson Phos-Chek began billowing from the belly of the airplane. 'This is it, one way or the other,' Matt thought as he dove to the ground, burying his face into the hot dirt and putting his arms over his head to hold his hard hat.

In the cockpit of Tanker Six One, the two pilots felt negative G-forces pulling them up, straining against their five-point harness as

Don pushed the nose over. When he could see the fire directly below him, he hit the red button on his control yoke, dropping the whole three thousand gallons all at once directly on the fire. Watching the bottom of the river canyon rushing up at him, he hauled back on the controls as hard as he could.

Fighting to pull the nose up while rolling the airplane to the right and kicking in the right rudder to turn downriver, he yelled to his copilot, "Get the gear up," while shoving all four throttles to the firewall. They felt positive G's smashing them back down into their seats.

Don held his breath as he tried to stay between the canyon walls. This was no place for an airliner, especially an old one.

Glancing nervously at the rock cliffs while bringing the flaps up in increments, his copilot sat quietly. He was used to this kind of crazy flying, and though he trusted Don completely, he briefly wondered about joining his brother in being a carpenter.

The retardant was still raining down when Captain Strand lifted his head to see if Tanker Six One would make it out of that canyon. The big DC-7 gently rolled upright as it leveled just above the river, its wingtips appearing to be mere feet from the embankment on either side of the shoreline. Finally, the nose came up and it started to climb.

Though retardant is not meant to put out fires, that much all at once served to snuff out most of the flames threatening the firefighters.

Don's accuracy was impeccable, but because the wind was blowing toward them, the Helitack crew got a big dose of retardant. They got up off the ground and looked around. The burned brush that seconds before had been a raging inferno was now hissing and smoking. The dry grass in the unburned terrain around them was painted red along with the backs of their yellow Nomex coveralls. There were seven little imprints of firefighters on the ground surrounded by red.

Matt looked at Gene and said, "Man, that was a close one."

Up in the Air Attack, Ranger Watson and I watched as Don Ornbaum turned and twisted that big ex-airliner through the narrow canyon as if he did it all the time. It was so low, the shadow of the airplane appeared glued to it.

When we could breathe again, Jerry said on the radio, "Good job, Six One. Tanker Six Zero, can you follow his drop?"

The pilot of Six Zero said, "Nope! I'm not doing that."

But Helitack was now safe. The danger was over. Six Zero could be used elsewhere.

The Temperate Flats fire was a big one. I flew on it for three days and logged twelve and a half hours. Aircraft and pilots were there from all over the state along with the heavy air tankers that the Forest Service loaned to us.

Ranger Watson and I, plus our two tankers from Columbia, spent two nights in Fresno while exchanging duties with the Fresno Air Attack plane. Someone was overhead all the time during daylight hours for three days.

Two days after we returned to Columbia, the ground firefighting crews were reporting it to be eighty percent contained, and no more aircraft were flying on it. Just to show how the news media would milk stories, when we turned on the television news, they were still showing footage of our tankers making drops. While the images had been taken three days prior, they were making it look like we were still out there fighting it. Meanwhile, we were sitting in our ready room and the airplanes were parked on the ramp.

Even back then, some called Don Ornbaum the John Wayne of tanker pilots. At six-foot-four, he was big, tough, and gruff. During World War II he flew both fighters and B-17 bombers. Since then he'd flown one of the B-25 bombers in the movie *Catch-22*. There was a story about him once meeting John Wayne. "The Duke" said to Don, "I hear you walk like me."

Don looked him in the eye and replied, "Well, I guess I'll just have to change the way I walk."

Wayne thought that was funny and they ended up becoming friends.

Three days later I was back at the Fresno base to pick up our regular Helitack 404 pilot, Wilson Granite, and deliver Wally Bracken, our relief helicopter pilot, to fill in. Entering the Fresno ready room, I saw Don Ornbaum sitting in one of the comfy lounge chairs, drinking a cup of coffee. Walking over, I plopped down into the overstuffed Naugahyde chair next to him.

In his deep voice, he said, "Hey, Dale, how ya doin'?"

I had met him briefly a few times and was taken aback that he remembered who I was.

"Hi, Don. I'm doin' good. Just came down to drop off Walley and pick up Wilson."

Muttering something about those crazy helicopter pilots, he reached into the zippered pocket on his Nomex flight suit and pulled out something, which he held out to me, saying, "Here, kid, I've got something for you."

Taking it, I saw it was an embroidered patch for the Fresno Air Attack Base with an image of a B-17 tanker making a drop.

I said, "Wow, that's cool. Thanks! Y'know, our Helitack crew was mighty impressed with that drop you made on them the other day."

He squinted a little and looked at me like it had been a long time ago and he was trying to recall. Then he slowly nodded and said, "Oh, yeah. Well, you can tell them they're lucky I didn't fall on them because I was completely out of control."

I chuckled, but he stared at me like he was totally serious.

I said, "In any case, they really appreciated it. They said you saved their lives."

Finally, a small smile pulled at the corners of his mouth. He said, "Tell them I said 'any time.'"

It really was like being in the presence of John Wayne, except he was an actor playing people like this. Don was the real deal.

The patch Don gave me.

A heartfelt thank you to retired CDF Battalion Chief Gene Strand for his input on this story.

It would be right to say that the helicopter's role in saving lives represents one of the most glorious pages in the history of human flight.

~Igor Sikorsky

Chapter 15
Helicopters

Helitack 404 at Columbia

Captain Strand stood on the skid of the big Huey tied to the helo with a makeshift strap of seatbelts. Ignoring the heat, the noise, and the blast of wind from the rotor blades overhead, he struggled to reach down to the firefighters as the fire raced up the mountainside below them.

The three men were standing on the roof of a fire engine directly underneath the hovering helicopter.

George was doing his best to hold a tight hover as the smoke from the oncoming flames roared up the steep slope. He felt like he was trying to hold the ship still over an erupting volcano. Right now, he and Captain Strand were the only chance these firefighters had.

And then the chilling vibration started…

***

Helicopter 404 had gotten into this tricky situation when a control burn got out of control – something that happened all too often. The fire engine's crew was now trapped on a hillside in what is called a chimney, which funnels a fire upward. It's a place you don't want to get caught in.

Gene and George had been asked to help these guys even though they weren't trained or equipped for this operation. They went in anyway and improvised.

They had to work fast. It was steep terrain with high, thick brush, and they couldn't get low enough to land and pick up the crew. That meant hovering over the fire truck was the only way. Over the radio, Gene told the crew to climb onto the top of the fire engine to get as high as they could. Then they could reach up to grab the skid, with Captain Strand to help them aboard.

Needing to hover into the wind, they had to face away from the terrain. That put the tail rotor in a gap between two clumps of thick brush on the side of the hill. Gene had to watch and tell the pilot what to do to keep the tail rotor out of the brush.

The two younger firefighters were able to climb aboard with no problem. A good dose of adrenaline probably helped them along.

The last one was the older, overweight CDF captain. He could grab hold of the skid but couldn't pull himself up. The helicopter could go no lower and time was running out.

Distracted by trying to help the captain, Gene wasn't able to watch the tail well enough.

Suddenly the helicopter started vibrating like an old Harley. Gene asked, "What's going on?"

Over the intercom, George said, "I'm getting a bad vibration in the pedals but no warning lights for the transmission. How does the tail look?"

Still straining to pull the captain up, Gene looked back. The aircraft looked normal, but some of the scrub oak around it had been mowed down like someone had taken a hedge trimmer to it.

Gene yelled into his boom mike, "It looks okay, but I think we've had a tail strike."

"I don't know how long that tail rotor will hold together, if it comes apart... Hurry up back there, would ya?"

Through the noise and wind from the rotors, Gene doubled his efforts, grabbing the captain by the wrists and pulling with all his might. He was able to pull the full-sized firefighter high enough so the other two could grab him and drag him into the crew compartment.

Gene yelled, "We're good. Let's get out of here."

George pulled some collective and eased the nose over into the canyon, not wanting to use the pedals any more than he had to.

Five minutes later they touched down in a field near the ground command post. They all breathed a sigh of relief as George shut down the engine.

The tail rotor was badly damaged, but the gear boxes and drive shafts were okay. If it had come off in the hover, they'd have spun into the mountainside, crashed, and rolled downhill into the fire. It's unlikely anyone would have survived.

Gene Strand and pilot George Johnson risked their lives that day to save those men. They had improvised and it worked. This is just one of the myriad examples of the usefulness of helicopters.

Weeks later, at a meeting, Gene and George were awarded the damaged tail rotor in a frame to hang on the wall in the Helitack office.

***

Aviation jobs were still hard to find. Knowing the Army didn't require a college degree to fly, I decided to sign up with the goal of flying helicopters. Something with guns on it – I wanted to fly the Apache, a badass flying tank!

In early 1982, while working in Santa Rosa during the off-season, I studied in my spare time and had just received my GED. Soon after, I walked into a recruiter's office and told him I wanted to enlist. When I told the sergeant I was a commercial pilot, he was enthusiastic. He asked me questions and filled out the form in front of him. I was scoring one hundred percent. Everything was going great until he asked if I'd ever been arrested. I told him the truth about my criminal record back when I was with the club.

He pushed back from his desk, broke his pencil in half, and threw it across the room, saying, "You've been wasting my time."

"But..." I protested, "I don't have any felony convictions."

"It doesn't matter. The way the government looks at it, if you were arrested for it, you did it."

"Isn't this the land of "innocent until proven guilty'?"

"Not as far as the government is concerned," he said.

"I thought when you got in trouble with the law, they gave you the choice of jail or joining the military."

"Yeah, they used to. That's how I got in. I was arrested for shooting at police helicopters during the Watts riots. I chose the Army, and it changed my life so much, I made a career out of it. Now everything is all-volunteer, and they've completely changed their standards."

I was only thirty years old and very fit, so I asked, "What about Rangers or Special Forces?"

He glared at me, shook his head, and said, "Get out of my office."

***

My admiration for helicopters wasn't quite enough for me to spend thousands of dollars that I didn't have to get qualified to fly them in the civilian world. I pushed that idea to the back of my mind. Besides, there were other goals.

I'd never flown in a helicopter, but one day in the '82 fire season, relief Helitack pilot Wally Bracken came to me and said, "Tomorrow I have to take the bird down to Stockton for some maintenance. Would you like to go along?"

I asked, "It's not for the tail rotor, is it?"

Knowing what had just happened, he chuckled and said, "No, it's for one of the radios."

"Okay. Tomorrow is my day off. That sounds great!"

He said, "I'll call in to headquarters and get permission to have you on board."

The next day I showed up at the helipad at the designated time. Wally was a Vietnam veteran, like the other helicopter pilots at Columbia. They'd faced an enemy that was constantly trying to kill them. It must have been a pleasure to fly every day with no one shooting at you.

Now the enemy wasn't "only" fire but also terrain, the wind, and the weather.

Wally put me in the left seat, as the pilot-in-command seat is normally on the right in helicopters. He was also a flight instructor and treated me like a student, which I thought was great. This wasn't just a ride. It was a lesson.

After explaining how the flight controls worked, he walked me through the engine start procedure, which seemed like a million things I couldn't possibly remember. It was my first experience with turbine engines, and I was enthralled.

My excitement spun up along with the whine of the turbine engine, and the big rotor blades started moving – slowly at first, then faster and faster.

Sitting on the helipad with the engine running and getting the transmission warmed up, the big rotor blades were whopping overhead just a few feet away. Wally ran the engine RPMs up to the required takeoff setting but still we sat there. It seemed so different from fixed-wing flying.

The aircraft was shaking from the rotors, and the engine was now a steady scream while the vibration was almost nonexistent. Checking all the gauges and seeing that everything looked good, he pulled up on the collective to change the pitch of the rotor blades. The ship floated straight up into the air.

He compensated with the anti-torque pedals to keep the nose pointed forward. To me, it felt magical, like how we dream of flying: smoothly floating up into the sky and going in any direction you want.

When you were young, did you dream of flying by rushing down a runway and flinging yourself into the air? I didn't. I dreamed of this.

We hovered higher until we were level with the tops of the tall pine trees. It was an amazing feeling. With the nose tilted down, we moved forward and started picking up speed as we went into translation, from hover to forward flight.

After accelerating down the runway, we climbed, and by the time we got to the southern end of the airport, Wally said, "You want to take it?"

He took me by surprise. Of course I did. I hadn't dared to think he'd let me fly this thing.

I just nodded as I put my hand on the "cyclic" control stick and my feet on the pedals. I didn't touch the collective because I had no clue how to operate it. I only knew it did the up-and-down stuff.

He told me to pick up Highway 49 and follow it as we turned westbound. We stayed about one hundred feet off the treetops. Some of the passengers and drivers of the cars on the road could be seen staring wide-eyed through their windshields at the big Huey. I couldn't believe I was flying this machine that had been such an icon of the Vietnam War.

In forward flight, the helicopter handled much like a fixed-wing airplane. Wally gave me instructions to "drive" it around, doing turns this way and that, picking up a compass heading or following a certain road. I loved it! The cockpit was at least twice the size of my O-2, and with the huge windshield, the visibility was great. He let me fly all the way to Stockton Airport until it was time to land.

My logbook says it was an hour and twelve-minute flight to Stockton, but it seemed mere minutes before we were there.

As we approached the airport, he took over the controls and expertly slowed and lowered us onto our parking spot at the CDF maintenance base. After stopping at the office to sign a couple of forms, we walked to the parking lot, where a rental car was waiting for us.

On the way out of town, we found a restaurant and had dinner. He answered all of my questions about helicopters and his time in Vietnam. He was happy to talk about helos but not the war.

A few hours later we were back at the Air Attack base at Columbia. Wally asked for my logbook and wrote an entry of dual instruction for the Bell UH-1F Huey.

At that moment I don't know why I didn't sell everything I owned, which wasn't much, to pay for rotary wing training and a helicopter license.

It was magical, rising into the air and floating down to land wherever you wanted, with no runway needed.

Here's another quote from Igor Sikorsky: "The helicopter is probably the most versatile instrument ever invented by man. It approaches closer than any other to fulfillment of mankind's ancient dream of the flying horse and the magic carpet."

***

I love helicopters. They hold a special place in aviation and are part of the mainstay of any aerial firefighting operation. They can do things that are impossible with fixed-wing aircraft. But they're more dangerous to fly.

Someone said, "An airplane is a flying machine, a helicopter is a machine that flies."

Here's a quote from journalist Harry Reasoner: "An airplane by its nature wants to fly, if not interfered with too strongly by unusual events or by a deliberately incompetent pilot, it will fly. A helicopter does not want to fly. It is maintained in the air by a variety of forces and controls working in opposition to each other, and if there is any disturbance in this delicate balance the helicopter stops flying; immediately and disastrously. There is no such thing as a gliding helicopter." (Maybe he didn't know about autorotation.)

The loss of helicopter pilots and firefighters (as passengers flying on fires) almost equals the number of tanker pilots. As I'm writing this in August 2023, just today we lost three more brave souls to a mid-air collision between two helicopters working a fire near Cabazon, California: a helicopter pilot, a Cal-Fire division chief who was the nephew of a close friend of mine, and a Cal-Fire captain. Fortunately, one of the helicopters was able to land safely.

Still, the stories of the lives being saved by helicopters are too numerous to count. Just look at the Vietnam War for an example.

I might be crazy, but at least I keep it interesting.

~Unknown

Chapter 16
Don't look down!

Standing on the skid outside the helicopter, I gulped in a deep breath as I gripped the surprisingly skinny rope with gloved hands, telling myself, "Don't freeze up." The furious rotor wash buffeted me, seemingly trying to knock me off the precarious little perch. If I were in an airplane, this would be low-leveling, but at this height, it felt like I was stepping outside the International Space Station.

I looked straight down beyond my firefighter boots toward the ground two hundred and fifty feet away. Immediately, I felt dizzy. The movie *Vertigo* suddenly came to mind.

The Navy crew chief yelled at me over the noise: "DON'T LOOK DOWN!"

'Too late,' I thought.

The noise was almost deafening. The shriek of the two turbine engines, combined with the growling whine of the transmission, echoed out of the almost empty crew compartment and through the open door of the U.S. Navy Huey. Mere feet over my head, the big rotor blades were whirling around, creating that hurricane downwash.

Working at the Columbia Air Attack Base wasn't all danger and risk. We had to have some fun whenever we could. They did say this would be fun, right?

***

Someone decided the Helitack crew should learn to rappel out of their helicopter. This would increase their capabilities so they could insert into areas where 404 couldn't land.

One morning, while strolling around the Helitack compound, killing time, I ran into Captain Gene Strand.

He said, "Hey, good news. The rappelling training has been approved. We'll be using the Navy's search and rescue bird out of Fallon, Nevada."

"Why not use 404?"

"There's a requirement to have two engines, and our old F model doesn't qualify."

"Oh, I see. That sounds awesome. When will it happen?"

"Next week, on Wednesday."

"I won't be here. I'm off that day."

Looking at me conspiratorially, he said, "How would you like to do the training with us?"

Not wanting to chicken out, I searched for excuses. "I did some repelling while mountain climbing in Alaska, but that was on the side of a mountain. I'm sure they wouldn't allow me to be part of your crew anyway."

Gene smiled and said, "Leave that to me."

Thinking it would never happen, I said, "Sounds great, count me in. How are you going to get the crew ready?"

"Don Stone and I have some mountaineering experience and we've rappelled a bunch of times. We're going to practice on the tower. It's only forty feet tall, so nobody has too far to fall if they mess it up."

I rolled my eyes. "Good idea. Nobody can get hurt falling only forty feet!"

"Well, it *is* over the lawn. We'll start tomorrow. Come and join us if you're not out flying."

Hoping I'd be out on a dispatch, I tried to sound confident. "Sure, I'll be there."

***

The next day at noon found me sitting in the Quonset hut ready room listening to the typical radio chatter on the loudspeaker. Gene stuck his head in the door and said, "We're about to start the training. You coming?"

No fires were reported anywhere, so with no excuses left, I wandered out onto the grass below the Air Attack tower. It had big windows on all sides and was full of radios and telephones and antennas on the roof. There was a metal staircase going up two sides and a balcony all around.

Practicing from Columbia Tower.

Gene and firefighter Don Stone were both on the Tuolumne County Search and Rescue Team and were already experts at this. They instructed all of us on how to wrap the harness around our waist and thighs, joining it at the front with a carabiner. We used a figure eight device to string the rope through and clamp it to the carabiner.

There are many knots and devices to use for rappelling, but I think the figure eight is the simplest and easiest to learn. Once you're locked onto the rope and wearing a pair of leather gloves, it's simply a matter of learning to control the speed of your descent and how to stop when you want to just hang there.

We spent hours dangling off the tower and sliding to the ground. It was a lot of fun.

On the appointed day the Helitack crew and I, led by Captain Strand, gathered at the general aviation parking area. The red and white Navy Search and Rescue helicopter swooped in and landed in the open area of dry grass on the west side of the runway.

After checking to make sure no airplanes were taking off or landing, Gene signaled us to go. We all jogged across the runway to meet them. I was dressed in a borrowed yellow Nomex suit, steel-toed firefighter boots, and a hard hat. Gene had snuck me in, so I blended in, pretending to be one of them. The Navy wouldn't let just anyone onto their aircraft.

As we got to the helo, the engines and rotors were winding down. Three people climbed out: a pilot or "aircraft commander," a copilot, and a crew chief.

They were very military and all business. The aircraft commander made a brief introduction, then turned it over to the crew chief to brief us on the requirements.

"We'll take up four at a time."

"Don't hook in until I tell you."

"Don't look down."

"Don't go too fast down the rope."

"Don't go too slow down the rope."

There were more instructions. I tried to remember them all. My life depended on it.

What really got my attention was when he said, "We'll be hovering at two hundred fifty feet."

My eyes widened and my mouth fell open. I thought we'd be going up just forty or fifty feet like we'd done off the tower the previous week. I wondered, "Do they even have ropes that long?"

I could have backed out, but that isn't my style. I took a bunch of deep breaths and boarded the helicopter when it was my turn, telling myself, "What the heck? I never thought I'd grow old anyway."

***

Back to the moment of truth: I stood on the skid in the whirlwind underneath the rotor blades.

Fighting off a wave of nausea, I wondered how I'd been dumb enough to get myself into this situation.

As instructed, I brought my eyes back to the crew chief inside the helicopter. My left hand held onto the vertical rope attached to the ship: my lifeline. Sticking my butt out while keeping my legs straight, I moved my right arm out to the side. The rope slid through my gloves as I sank farther away from the relative safety of the crew compartment. There was no turning back now.

The crew chief was pointing downward yelling, "GO, GO, GO!"

So, I went, went, went. Moving my right hand outward, I fed the rope through the figure eight device, then sank down until I was completely upside down with my feet still on the bottom of the skid, as we'd been trained to do. As I let out more rope, my boots left the skid. I swung upright to a sitting position and dropped free from that big whining wind machine, then started sliding away into space.

Being so close to the hovering ship was quite a sight, but I had no free hands with which to take a picture. The crew chief was leaning out the door watching me. Working the rope with my right hand as the brake, I started the long descent to the ground. I kept thinking, 'Damn, this rope sure is skinny.'

Despite being told not to look down, I did. I was fascinated by how far it looked. Now that I was there, hanging from a rope in mid-air, it was an incredible feeling. Or maybe it was just the adrenaline.

As instructed, I tried not to go too fast, as doing so would heat up the figure eight device. Then something odd happened: A calm feeling came over me and the fear was gone. Maybe it was that near-death thing. I just wanted to hang there for a while and look around. I *was* having fun after all.

But I couldn't dally, as more firefighters needed their time on the rope. Each of us got to do this only once. I'm sure the crew chief was swearing at me for taking so long.

The faces of the other firefighters came into focus as the ground got closer. Finally, my feet touched the earth again. I let out enough slack, unhooked the carabiner, and undid the rope from the figure eight device. As I turned to walk to the group of assembled firefighters, Gene was suddenly by my side. Over the noise, he yelled, "How did it go?"

"That was great. Can I do it again?"

He laughed and said, "Sorry, pal. Only one time is needed for qualification."

I shook my head and said, "Damn, I don't think I'm qualified yet."

I never got to use my "qualification" to rappel out of a helicopter, but it was fun nonetheless. How many people get to do that?

The '82 fire season was longer than normal, lasting until the middle of October. Dropping off my O-2 in Santa Rosa, I was off again in search of permanent employment. I'd take anything I could get as long as it was in an airplane.

Starting the long slide down the rope. Photo: Retired Ranger Gene Strand.

Any job worth doing is worth doing well.

~My father

Chapter 17
The itinerant pilot

The wonderful old DC-3

In the off-season, I got a part-time job taking up skydivers: crazy people who love to jump out of perfectly good airplanes. One of the cool things about that was getting to be a copilot on the ancient DC-3, an absolute classic. Even then, it was a piece of history, designed in the 1930s by American Airlines president C. R. Smith working with the Douglas Aircraft Company.

A big, slow, swan of an airplane, it was rugged and dependable. As with any taildragger, you had to be on your toes, literally, on the rudders for takeoff and landing. When you were sitting in the cockpit on the ground with its nose in the air, it felt like you were twenty-five feet off the ground. The big twelve-hundred-horsepower radial engines snarled and vibrated, making you feel like the airplane had a life of its own.

The C-47 version was a workhorse for the military in World War II and was still being used as late as the Vietnam War.

A type rating was required to be the pilot-in-command because it weighed more than twelve thousand five hundred pounds. Having a type rating would help me get a job in an air tanker, where the good money was.

I'd been checked out earlier in the year by Chief Pilot Howie Bohl. I was already an official DC-3 copilot for Perris Airport Skydivers. I made several takeoffs and landings that day, and it was always a thrill getting to fly that airplane.

One day in December I was flying with a captain named Steve. We were doing hops in the DC-3, taking skydivers up to fourteen thousand feet, kicking them out, and then diving back to the runway.

As we climbed, I yelled over the noise of the engines, "How can I get a type rating in this thing?"

Steve said, "I know a designee who can do it for you, and I'm a CFI. Have you got twelve hundred dollars?"

"No, but I think I can get it. When can we start?"

"We'll need to do it soon because this airplane has been sold to an outfit in Florida. In fact, I'm leaving on Sunday to ferry it down there and I'm going to need a copilot. Want to go along?"

"Absolutely!"

I borrowed the money from my old buddy and fellow pilot, Tom. The next day I showed up at Perris Airport and, after a rigorous and detailed preflight, Steve and I took off to begin my instruction. We performed engine-out procedures, stalls, and steep turns, then went to Hemet-Ryan Airport for touch and goes. Hemet was kind of my home airport, where I still did some instructing, so flying around the pattern in that big DC-3 was a treat. The flight time was only two hours, with five landings.

When we landed back at Perris, Steve handed me an operating manual and said, "Take this home and study as much as you can. I'll see you back here tomorrow."

The next morning, in just under an hour, we flew N87640 to Camarillo Airport in Ventura, where we met Harry Patton, the FAA designee. Without shutting the engines down, I parked the brakes while Steve went back and opened the door. Harry climbed aboard and we shook hands. Steve climbed back into the copilot's seat while our check airman sat in the tiny jump seat. Off we went.

The check ride was straightforward. I did everything Steve had trained me on the day before. The airplane was pretty easy to fly, and after forty-eight minutes Harry called it good, saying I'd passed. I was now qualified to be pilot-in-command of this big old bird that was older than I was. It was my first type rating, and I felt like a real pilot. Maybe I could find a job flying one of these.

We dropped Harry off at the gas pumps, then filled the long-range tanks and pointed her eastbound.

In deference to my new type rating, Steve let me fly in the left seat, the captain's chair.

Climbing to eleven thousand five hundred feet, we called air traffic control and got "flight following" for our VFR flight plan as we followed the San Angeles mountain range to the east. With the Los Angeles basin on our right, the population centers eventually thinned out, giving way to the great American desert.

The DC-3 rumbled along confidently as I fantasized about what it would have been like to be an airline pilot in the 1930s or 1940s, having a load of passengers in the back and maybe a young, pretty stewardess.

Five hours after departing Ventura we touched down in Fort Stockton, Texas. We lost two hours with the time zone, and it was now almost dark. After getting a ride to a motel with a diner out front, we grabbed a bite to eat and got a good night's sleep.

In the morning, while ordering breakfast, we had a hard time understanding the accent of the waitress. Neither of us spoke Texan. We finally figured out she was recommending the biscuits and gravy, so we gave that a try and weren't disappointed. Back at the airport with full bellies and full tanks, we were soon climbing into a high overcast sky.

Once again, we were at our preferred cruising altitude of eleven thousand five hundred feet. With a good tailwind, we crossed just north of Houston two hours later. It was surprising to me how green this part of Texas was after the arid terrain of West Texas.

Crossing the shoreline, we left the land behind as we flew over the Gulf of Mexico. Steve said, "Come farther right about fifteen degrees until the Cypress VOR comes in. Then we'll head straight for Fort Lauderdale."

"Shouldn't we stay closer to shore in case of an engine failure?"

"Naw, we'll be fine. This ol' girl will fly forever on one engine."

We passed south of New Orleans. Out the left window, we could see the city in the distance, along with the lush green peninsula of the Pass a Loutre Wildlife Area.

It was December 1982 and we were lucky to have none of the volatile weather of the warmer months – no rain squalls or towering thunderstorms with flashing lightning.

As we droned along over the Gulf of Mexico, there was nothing but water as far as we could see. However, I was comfortable trusting basic navigation. That was how I learned to fly, and besides, it would have been hard to miss the whole state of Florida. I'd never flown over this much water before. I worried about the gas and kept computing the fuel on board, along with the distance, the time, and the fuel used per hour.

I said, "I think it's going to be close. Maybe we should land at Fort Myers."

"Naw, we'll be alright. We're empty, and this bird has long-range tanks."

"We're about three hours out and we have three hundred and fifty gallons. At about one hundred gallons per hour, that leaves only fifty gallons when we land."

"We also have a tailwind and we'll use less as we descend. Fifty gallons will be fine. That's over half an hour of reserves in VFR conditions. Relax."

I tried to relax, but the Gulf of Mexico felt like the Pacific Ocean to me. The thick, humid air, even in December, prevented you from seeing more than about fifty miles at a time.

Eventually the west coast of the Florida peninsula came into view. Air traffic control called us "radar contact" and told us to maintain five thousand feet.

After we crossed the shoreline just south of Fort Myers, we saw the lush green Everglades. The reflection of water shined up through the ever-present swampy grasses, which seemed endless.

To keep us under the Miami arrivals and departures, ATC kept stepping us down, lower and lower. We saw the occasional airboat blasting along the canals through the sea of grass. I scanned for alligators but never saw any.

A couple of the airboat drivers looked up and waved as we went over. We were lower than expected and were using more fuel than planned.

Up ahead was the deep blue of the Atlantic Ocean. As we got closer to the airport, the Everglades gave way to houses, streets, and commercial buildings underneath us. We were lined up on runway 10 right at Fort Lauderdale.

I realized I'd been holding my breath. Glancing nervously at the fuel gauges, I could see we were going to make it. I breathed a sigh of relief as the tower cleared us to land.

Despite my self-imposed stress, I managed to make a decent wheel landing, and we stopped with plenty of room to spare.

Ground control cleared us to taxi to an FBO at the west end of the airport. There, a line boy guided us into a parking place and gave the signal to shut down. When the mixtures were pulled off, the propellers clicked slower and slower into silence. The now-quiet airplane felt like it was receding into the past where it belonged. Or maybe it was just me.

We'd accomplished our mission and it felt great. I checked the Hobbs meter and entered it into my logbook: seven hours and thirty minutes since leaving Fort Stockton.

Stepping down the ladder and onto this part of the country marked the first time I'd been back to Florida since my family left in 1959: twenty-three years before. I'd forgotten how warm and humid it could be. Christmas was right around the corner.

Steve went into the FBO to pay for the airplane's parking and arrange a courtesy car into town.

The hotel wasn't expensive, nor was it that clean, and we couldn't see the ocean. However, we could smell the salty air, and the warm breeze was intoxicating as we sat on the open-air patio of a restaurant next door and ordered mojitos.

I stuck with a standard Cubano sandwich, while Steve had something more exotic that I couldn't pronounce. After an adequate number of drinks, we called it a day.

I was so relieved the airplane kept running and the fuel had lasted. When I got to my room, I was asleep before my head hit the pillow.

Steve and the DC-3 in Fort Lauderdale.

All you need in this life is ignorance and confidence; then success is sure.

~Mark Twain

Chapter 18
Once again, better lucky than good

The telephone next to my bed jarred me out of a sound sleep. As soon as I opened my eyes, I felt a little hungover.

Steve's voice said, "The buyer of the airplane wants it delivered to Tamiami Airport today, so we need to get out to the airport and get that done this morning. I have a flight back to California this afternoon."

"I'll see you in the lobby in fifteen minutes."

He said, "I'll call a cab."

Back at the airplane, Steve said, "The gauges say we have fifty gallons, twenty-five in each wing. That's not much and most of it will be used on takeoff. I'm not sure about these gauges. They're over forty years old. I don't want to have too little, but I don't want to put on too much fuel. That comes out of my pocket. I figure we'll use about thirty-five gallons, enough to take off and land at Tamiami Airport. I don't want to land with fifteen gallons. That's too tight."

"Yeah, fifty gallons would be minimal," I said.

"Right. We'll stick the tanks and make sure we know exactly how much fuel is in there. That way I won't put too much on. It'd be a waste of money."

Steve had a calibrated wooden stick with lines and numbers on it. After climbing on the wings, he unscrewed the fuel caps and stuck the stick into the tanks, then carefully wrote down the numbers.

When finished, he consulted a chart in the airplane's operating manual, which like the fuel gauges, was over forty years old.

Steve sat in the back door, his feet hanging out into the warm Florida breeze. He paled when he looked up from the chart at me with an expression I can describe only as shock or disbelief.

I said, "What's wrong?"

"Like I suspected, those old gauges are wrong. We don't have fifty gallons on board. We have about twenty. A little over ten gallons in each side. The tanks are almost dry. If we'd had to go around, the engines would have quit."

The realization hit me too. We'd flown over the Gulf of Mexico, past the west coast of Florida, across miles of Everglades full of alligators and snakes, and then over the populated area of Fort Lauderdale with houses, buildings, and busy streets, never realizing how little gas we had. We'd been on fumes when we landed.

Despite the warm air, I suddenly felt cold. We were both silent as it sank in how lucky we had been, lulled into complacency by erroneous fuel gauges. Still, if we'd crashed, it wouldn't have been the airplane's fault. It would have been ours. If we'd taken off again thinking we had fifty gallons, we wouldn't have made it.

Steve ordered fifty gallons of gas, to be safe. We'd have seventy gallons for takeoff: thirty-five per side for the twenty-four-minute ride to Tamiami Airport. We'd use about half.

The short, low-level flight from Fort Lauderdale to Tamiami was uneventful. We took off to the east, and the view was breathtaking as we climbed over the white-sand beaches full of tourists. The deep blue of the Atlantic Ocean and an azure sky full of puffy white clouds contrasted with the gleaming buildings of downtown Miami twenty miles to the south.

I would have loved to have cruised down the coast at low level, but we had to avoid the jets flying into and out of Miami International. However, ATC told us to make a left one-eighty, and we flew back across the populated areas until we were once again over the emerald-green Everglades.

Then we turned south, rumbling along at twenty-five hundred feet with those big radial engines on either side of us. I was thoroughly enjoying the experience, not knowing when I'd fly a DC-3 again.

After landing, we taxied in and parked in a grass parking area. A line boy showed up with a golf cart and we unloaded our gear and flight bags. Then he drove us to the FBO.

The author in Fort Lauderdale. Last leg in the DC-3.

Steve met with the new owners, signed some papers, and collected the payment for the ferry flight.

He came over and handed me two hundred dollars in cash. It was my pay for the ferry flight, enough for a plane ticket back to California.

He said, "Thanks for your help. I'm getting a ride to Miami International. Are you coming?"

"No, thanks, I'll get a ride to the rental car place. I haven't been back here since I was a kid and it'll be nice to take a couple of days to look around. It's been a pleasure flying with you. I'll see you around."

We shook hands and parted. That was the last time I ever saw him.

I spent the next four days driving around south Florida, staying in the cheapest motels I could find and visiting places I remembered from when I was a kid, like the Coral Castle, with its carvings from solid coral, all made by one man. It has been called Florida's Stonehenge.

On the Dixie Highway, I found the Miami Serpentarium, with its huge thirty-five-foot-tall statue of a cobra out front. Back in the fifties, it had been out of town, surrounded by palm trees. Now I was surprised to find it on a busy street between a bank and a McDonald's.

The Miami Serpentarium in the fifties.

They were still putting on demonstrations milking all kinds of poisonous snakes for their venom, including king cobras, mambas, and kraits. I bought a ticket and went in. It was still a thrill to be within feet of those deadly creatures as Dr. Haast handled them.

Stopping in my old town of Homestead, I got a motel room and had dinner at McDonald's. Rather than sit indoors and listen to the loud air conditioner, I went out for a walk to enjoy the atmosphere of the cooler night.

Walking in the grass on the side of Highway 1, I came upon an estate where the house was set way back from the road. It had a chain link fence at least ten feet tall, and on the other side of that fence were four *very* large Great Danes.

It was late, it was dark, and when they saw me, they started to bark. Sounding for all the world like Cerberus, they scolded me as I strolled by.

I felt confident with that ten-foot fence between us, so, to entertain myself, I started trying to imitate their throaty growls – up until the point I realized that one of them, the biggest it seemed, was on **my** side of the fence and was advancing stiff-legged toward me!

The realization sent ice water through my veins. My brain raced for a solution.

How stupid could I be, provoking dogs that probably weighed more than I did?

I shifted gears from provoking mode to pacification mode or "don't kill me" mode.

Then I tried changing to "master" mode, trying to talk like a dog trainer who was in command.

Speaking to the Great Dane on the outside of the fence in the deepest voice I could muster, I said, "Stay, sit! Good boy!" I had no idea what to say, but I knew it wasn't a good time to insult his lineage.

He didn't sit, but he did stay.

I was eternally grateful that he didn't come and tear my throat out. That would have been very hard to recover from.

They continued barking until I was a block away. I walked for another six blocks before I got the nerve to head back to the motel – this time, of course, on the other side of the street.

On my way back, they were no longer there, including the big guy that had been outside the fence. I didn't know where he went. Back to the gates of hell, I expect.

Like dodging the bullet on running out of gas in the DC-3, I felt like I'd dodged death by dog.

(Wikipedia says the average yearly "death by dog" is thirty to fifty, with the majority being adults. About four and a half million Americans are bitten every year, resulting in hospitalizations from dog attacks of six thousand to thirteen thousand per year.)

The next day I hunted down the tiny two-bedroom house where my family of six had lived outside Homestead. It was still in a very rural area surrounded by farmland and nurseries. It had seemed so big when I was five years old.

Key Largo and Key West were just as I remembered them. It was magical to see them as an adult so many years later. My whole visit to Florida was like that: perfect weather with lush greenery and blue skies. I almost wanted to move back there.

It was time well spent, but all too soon I had to get on a commercial flight and head home.

Twenty-three years had passed since my family left Florida in a 1955 Ford Fairlane to drive to California. It seemed like a lifetime. Now, as I write this, forty-one more years have passed. It seems like several lifetimes ago.

It's no wonder most of the airplanes I've flown are in museums.

The only difference between where you are and where you want to be is the steps you haven't taken yet.

~ Rigel J. Dawson

Chapter 19
Getting a Ph.D. without going to college

In April 1983, I saw an ad from a flight training operation at Orange County Airport, offering a jet type rating in a Cessna Citation for six thousand dollars. They also had a program for a Learjet type rating, which I wanted even more, but at ten thousand dollars, it cost almost twice as much, and for someone who'd never flown jets, it was harder to fly. Lears have been described as being "unforgiving."

I'd already passed the written test for the ATP, or Airline Transport Pilot. The same qualification airline captains must have, it is the highest pilot rating and is sometimes called the "Ph.D. of flying." I hoped this new rating would help me find a real job, only this time flying jets.

I went to my bank in Hemet and asked for a personal loan of six grand. Surprisingly they gave it to me with no collateral. That was a lot more than I'd paid for my car. I called Orange County Aviation and scheduled the training.

The Citation was a dream to fly and certainly the most modern and high-performance aircraft for me to date. The same size as a Lear, although not as fast and the long, straight wing made it easier to handle.

The training was intense. In the back of my logbook, I wrote down all the maneuvers and practice approaches, almost always on one engine. Even with abbreviations, it took up almost a whole page.

This particular airplane was a CE-501 SP, which stands for "single pilot." Unlike most jets, it could be flown by one person.

With the same Pratt & Whitney turbofan engines of the T-37 Air Force trainer, it was quiet and smooth. The flight instruments were very modern, with vertical tape engine gauges, a panel of red and yellow warning lights, and a flight director. This, of course, was before cathode ray tube (CRT) display screens, at least in smaller airplanes.

After four training hops and six flight hours in four days, I was ready to take the check ride – or at least they said I was.

The author at the controls of the Citation. I'd finally gotten rid of the beard from my biker days.

Flying the airplane itself was easy, but the check ride was not. Doing instrument departures on one engine and making engine out approaches under the hood was hard work. Everything went fine until I turned the wrong way on an outbound NDB approach and the check airman busted me.

I was devastated. Not for the first time, I wondered if I was up to a career flying jets. As an instrument instructor, I taught this stuff to students, and I was mortified at making a mistake like that. The check airman encouraged me not to worry about it, to relax, take a week off, and rest up, but I insisted on coming back the next day.

After another two-hour drive back to the airport, we were at it again. Flying an engine out ILS, then a VOR approach, I aced the NDB approach and passed, getting not only a Citation type rating, but my airline transport rating as well. My self-confidence was restored.

Feeling highly qualified now, I started looking for a job as a copilot flying Citations or anything else I could find. However, the economy had yet to pick up and flying jobs were still scarce.

I would have moved anywhere in the country and lived in a cardboard box if someone had offered me a job flying the Citation. I called every jet charter outfit I could find, but when they asked about my flight time, they said it was still too low, even with the required fifteen hundred hours for the ATP rating.

***

In May 1983 I was about to head back to Columbia for my third season in Air Attack 440. Something I saw on the news got my attention. Golden West, a commuter airline in Southern California, was going out of business.

Knowing another company would probably take up the slack, I found out their competitor was Imperial Airlines. After getting the number of their office from the phone book I gave them a call.

A pleasant female voice answered. I asked, "Are you hiring pilots?"

She said, "Yes, we are. Applicants must have an Airline Transport Rating."

"For copilots?" Even first officers at American or United Airlines weren't required to have that.

"Yes, we want our copilots to be able to move to the left seat when the time comes."

"Well, it just so happens I do have an ATP."

Then she said, "It pays six dollars and twenty-eight cents per flight hour. If you come down here to our headquarters at Palomar Airport tomorrow morning, our HR department will be doing interviews."

"I'll be there."

I was excited. This was my biggest opportunity yet. Showing up at eight the next morning, I was directed to a waiting room with ten other pilots already there.

The pilot pecking order was in progress, as we each determined what kind of experience and qualifications the others had. Of course, we all had ATPs, and I felt pretty smug with my two type ratings – one of them in a jet – until I heard that a couple of these guys had been flying C-141 cargo planes in the Air Force. Four-engine jets! Another had been a Marine Corps C-130 pilot, and another had been an NFO, or naval flight officer (back-seater), in F-14 Tomcats. Wow, flying jobs really were hard to come by.

Someone told a funny story about an applicant asking the lady doing the interviews, "At six dollars and twenty-eight cents an hour, how do you expect someone to live on so little money?"

Her answer was, "Don't your parents help you out?"

Her father owned the company.

The interview went well. I didn't mention the money and answered all of her questions. I was happy when she didn't ask, "Have you ever been arrested?"

It wasn't long before it was over and she said, "Thank you, we'll let you know."

I figured "That's that." I was sure I didn't have a chance against those military pilots. At least I probably still had my summer job flying on the fires. I drove home and tried to forget about it.

A week later I was listening to Chief Pilot Harry Chaffee's voice on the phone say, "I've got your seat at Columbia again this year if you want it."

"I'll take it, but are there any tanker seats open this year? I have two type ratings and an ATP now."

He said, "That's great, congratulations, but no, sorry."

"That's okay. It will be good to get back to Columbia."

Once again, Harry said, "This is no business for a young guy like you. You should get a real job." It was becoming his mantra.

Harry was a gruff guy with a reputation for being a hard case. However, I think because so many pilots had been lost over the years, he didn't want me to be one of those sad statistics, like my friend Jim Aiken.

Two weeks later I was back in Columbia with Norm and JD, getting settled into my third fire season. One afternoon we were lounging in the ready room when the phone rang. Norm answered it: "Columbia Ready Room." Then he looked at me and held out the phone.

"Hello, this is Dale."

"Hi, Dale. This is Steve Amoia with Imperial Airlines. It wasn't easy tracking you down, but someone at the number you left said you'd be here. How would you like to come to work for us? We have a class starting on Thursday."

Almost speechless, I stammered, "Uh… yeah… Thursday? What time?"

"Eight-thirty."

It was Monday! So much for giving two weeks' notice. I said, "I'll be there."

Hanging up, I immediately called Harry: "I'm sorry, boss, but I just got offered a job with a commuter in Southern California and they need me there on Thursday."

Harry didn't seem upset. He said, "Good for you. I'll have the relief Air Attack pilot there in the morning and he'll fill in for you until we get a replacement. I've got a list of people here who want that job. Good luck."

I think he was glad I was following his advice.

Greatly relieved, I thanked him profusely and hung up. My mind was reeling as I ran around telling the good news to the other pilots, the CDF staff, and my friends in the Helitack unit.

We weren't dispatched for the rest of the day, and I could hardly wait for the six o'clock release time to run back to the trailer and pack.

Just before leaving the base, I went out to the Air Attack ramp where our airplanes were parked. Sitting in the O-2, I quietly said goodbye, knowing I'd probably never fly it again. We'd been through a lot of adventures in the last three years. I'd taken care of her, and she'd taken care of me.

That evening Norm, JD, some of the firefighters, and I had some beers in a little farewell get-together. They said they'd all miss me but were happy for me and my new opportunity in my journey as a professional pilot.

Bright and early the next morning I was off with what few belongings I had, driving southbound, filled with excitement about the new adventure awaiting me.

My flying career had found new wings.

I think, therefore I am... dangerous.

~Unknown

Chapter 20

A few thoughts before we leave the aerial firefighting business behind

Twin-engine aircraft are great because they will fly on one engine if the other one quits. Or do they? Well… not always.

I've talked previously about how an engine failure must be handled very carefully or else the asymmetric thrust can roll the airplane over on its back. If you're at low altitude that's a very bad thing.

The O-2A and its civilian cousin, the Cessna 337, don't have that problem because the engines are both mounted on the centerline. No asymmetric thrust to ruin your day. However, there are other issues. With any "light" twin, there's the problem of density altitude. (See the aviation glossary at the back of this book.)

If you lose an engine in an O-2A at its gross takeoff weight, it will maintain only fifteen hundred feet above sea level. At Columbia, on a ninety-degree day, the density altitude would be four thousand five hundred feet, which is three thousand feet higher than the airplane would want to fly on one engine.

Simply put, you'd have to start heading downhill fast and hope nothing got in your way before the airplane held enough altitude to get you to an airport.

The O-2A had long-range tanks, so it could stay in the air for a long time if needed. However, we never used them because they made the airplane too heavy. Even without the extra fuel, it might not have stayed in the air on one engine.

I was very fortunate in that I never lost an engine on takeoff out of Columbia. However, a few years after I left, that very thing happened to another pilot and his Ranger passenger.

The front engine quit shortly after takeoff, and even with full power on the rear engine, they couldn't hold their altitude. They were already too low to get back to Columbia.

The altimeter kept unwinding without mercy, and it became obvious they wouldn't be able to make an airport at Modesto or Stockton. Accepting the inevitable, the pilot spotted an empty field and headed for it.

Leaving the gear up, the pilot bellied the plane into the dirt field and kept it upright as they quickly slid to a stop. He did a great job. They were both okay as they climbed out and waited for the helicopter from Columbia to come and get them. That airplane never flew again.

***

A brief history of the economics of the aerial firefighting business in the 1980s

We used to say that flying on the fires was "like flying in combat, only nobody was shooting at you."

I later modified that to say, "only nobody was trying to kill you, except maybe the company you worked for."

There's a story about the early astronauts in the Apollo program. Alan Shepard said, "I realized I was sitting on top of a rocket that was built by the lowest bidder."

That's the way it was with the aerial firefighting program in California in the 1980s. Companies competed for contracts from the state, and the contracts went to the lowest bidder. Everything was done on a shoestring: pilot pay and especially aircraft maintenance. On top of that, the fact that you had a contract one year didn't guarantee you'd get a contract the next year. Aircraft received little to no maintenance in the winter because if the company didn't get another contract, the cost of the work and parts would be wasted, and the company could go bankrupt.

The California Department of Forestry leased the O-2s from the Air Force and the S-2s from the Navy for one dollar. The contractor won by putting in the lowest bid for an hourly rate. Now he had to make them flyable and keep them that way throughout the season while also providing a pilot (or pilots), maintenance, and fuel.

All companies need to make a profit to stay in business. If there's no profit, what's the point? The more profit, the better. However, where does that fine line end when the profit is made off people's lives?

Flying into fires at low altitude, in high heat and low visibility, in thirty-year-old airplanes, is dangerous enough without cutting corners on maintenance.

There's a process for aircraft engines called TBO, which stands for "time before overhaul." The manufacturer sets the recommended maximum time, and the FAA approves it. An engine can go longer if it passes inspection, but it's on borrowed time. However, the CDF aircraft were not operated under commercial FAA regulations. They were operated by the state.

The U.S. Navy would operate an engine on the S-2 for two thousand hours, then, figuring that was the limit, they'd take it off and store it in the "bone yard." The taxpayers would pay for a new one.

I was told back then that the cost to rebuild a Wright R-1820 nine-cylinder Cyclone engine for an S-2 in 1981 was thirty-six thousand dollars. However, the contractor could get a runout, two-thousand-hour engine from the Navy for nothing.

When an S-2 pilot flying on fires lost an engine, the company replaced it with a two-thousand-hour engine from the "bone yard." All it cost the company was to pay the mechanics to change it.

The tanker pilot then flew off to his next mission with a two-thousand-hour engine, confronting smoke, heat, downdrafts, high terrain, and obstacles all around – and that two-thousand-hour engine… was the "new" one.

The whole system back then seemed to be designed to get pilots killed. I believe they did the same thing with the O-2s that I flew, but the Air Attacks weren't doing the hazardous job that the tankers were.

Because the companies didn't own the airplanes, they couldn't insure them. When a plane crashed, the company got nothing.

There was a scandal back in the 1980s. The owner of at least one company took out life insurance policies on the pilots: fifty thousand dollars, double indemnity. When a pilot died, the company (the owner) collected one hundred thousand dollars.

A nice way to offset those lowest-bidder contracts, wouldn't you say?

Gotta love those run-out engines.

***

In memory of the air tanker pilots I knew and those I didn't.

A DC-6 making a drop of Phos check retardant.

Jim Aiken died in 1982 in his second year flying an S-2.

Ted Bell, crashed while flying on a fire in 1984. He was the newest S-2 pilot.

That same year Ed Real crashed and died. He was one of the most experienced S-2 pilots.

Grass Valley-based Roger Stark died in 1992, also flying an S-2. Grass Valley is just north of Columbia.

In 1998 I read a newspaper story about an air tanker crashing in New Mexico. The pilot was Jerry "JD" Donahue, in a P2V.

Also, in 1998 Captain Gary from the Ted Bell story died in a crash while fighting a fire in an S-2 in Southern California. Six pilots died that year.

Below is a link to the Airtanker.org memorial wall of those who have died in their airplanes and helicopters while trying to protect people and homes on the ground.

They were doing what they loved, and we love them for doing it.

While collecting information for this chapter, I found a shocking statistic: From 1958 to 2002, one hundred and thirty-six tanker pilots died on the job.

That's an average of just over three per year.

Since 2002 there have been fifty-four more, not including 2023. As of this writing, there have already been three more in California.

The worst year was 2020, with nine deaths from seven accidents. Keep in mind this is only in the United States. It happens in other parts of the world too. This year in Greece, one tanker crashed, killing two, while another in Australia killed three. It was a U.S. crew.

It isn't the most dangerous job in the world… or is it? When you consider the low number of people doing it, I have to wonder.

This list grows every year.

https://airtanker.org/memorial/

Change your thoughts and you can change your world.
~Norman Vincent Peale

Chapter 21
Imperial Airlines, working for a living

Thursday morning found me sitting in a classroom at Palomar Airport in Carlsbad, California. It was less than a mile from the Pacific Ocean and the same location where I'd had the interview six weeks prior.

Twenty-five other pilots were in the room, and we found out we weren't really hired… yet.

This was a ground school, then there would be an aircraft checkout. You had to pass both before you were hired.

Once again, there were a lot of highly qualified pilots. I thought, 'Maybe I shouldn't have quit my job with Sys-Q so fast…'

We'd be learning everything there was to know about the Brazilian-made Embraer EMB-110 Bandeirante. They called it the "Bandit."

It was a twin-engine turboprop. The engines were Pratt and Whitney PT-6 turbines instead of pistons.

If I was selected, I'd be building up valuable "turbine time." The aircraft held eighteen passengers and, at gross weight, weighed just under twelve thousand five hundred pounds. No special type rating was required.

The Bandit had a simple and rugged design with no auxiliary power unit, or APU. It was unpressurized, so we never went above ten thousand feet. It didn't even have an autopilot. Why have an autopilot when you were paying two pilots to fly it?

Steve Amoia was the chief pilot, and he instructed the class which lasted all day, there was a written test at the end. Those who passed would be asked to come back in a couple of days for a checkout in the Bandeirante.

At the end of the day Steve thanked us for our time and said we'd be getting a phone call in a day or two.

I suspect some who passed the ground school weren't offered a job – people like the loudmouth who was always interrupting and asking dumb questions or wanting to tell his own anecdotal stories.

Steve might have chosen people as much on character and personality as on pilot experience or ability. I think he wanted to see who'd fit into a cockpit environment.

On the two-hour drive back to my mother's apartment, I felt I'd made a big mistake. Flying jobs were hard to come by in the early 1980s and I'd just walked out on one for the uncertainty of being chosen out of a roomful of other pilots. On the way, I stopped and bought a newspaper so I could check the want ads for pilot jobs.

The next day I'd just walked in the door after my morning run when the phone rang. I answered it.

"Hi, Dale. This is Steve Amoia. Can you be at Palomar tomorrow at nine o'clock for your Bandeirante checkout?"

I was surprised and excited but restrained myself from jumping up and down when I said, "Absolutely, I'll be there."

I was elated knowing I'd passed the hurdle of ground school. Now I'd get to fly the airplane. I knew I could do that part.

Saturday morning found me once again at Palomar Airport, walking through the front door of the Imperial Airlines headquarters. The receptionist directed me to the hangar, where I found Steve and a small group of pilots from the class. I was surprised there were only a dozen of us.

I wondered what had happened to the other thirteen but didn't ask any questions. I was just happy to be there.

After an in-depth explanation of how to do a walk-around inspection, Steve chose one of the new guys to sit in the right seat for takeoff. The rest of us loaded into the back like passengers. Spirits were high as we chatted among ourselves.

Once airborne, we flew to a practice area where he trained the first guy. Then we each rotated into the right seat while Steve flew.

The checkout in the Bandit was pretty straightforward. It was built like a truck, and it felt like one: heavy on the controls and taking a lot of force to manipulate. The cockpit had seven windows, enhancing that "big airplane" feel. Best of all, it was a turboprop. It was almost as good as flying jets!

We were tested on our ability to control the airplane with steep turns and approach-to-stalls, then the ever-important single-engine work. Finally, we went back to Palomar to do some touch and goes, three for each of us.

A funny characteristic of the Bandit was that when you went to full flaps for landing, the nose pitched down dramatically, and you needed to pull back hard on the control yoke to overcome it. I heard the only reason it needed two pilots was because the forces were so strong that sometimes the control yoke would break off just before landing and there had to be someone else to take over when that happened. However, I don't know if that's true.

On the ground at Palomar, Steve gathered us outside the airplane and told us we'd all done well. We were now qualified as second in command and, best of all, we were finally hired. He gave us the address of a clothing store in San Diego where we were to get fitted for uniforms. Of course, we'd have to pay for them ourselves.

They told us at the interview that the pay was a lofty six hundred and twenty-eight dollars per month before taxes. That was assuming you flew one hundred hours per month. My mother made more than that on Social Security.

Today, FAA regulations no longer allow for flying that much per month, but most of us did that and more. It wasn't unusual to fly one hundred and twenty or thirty hours per month and eight days in a row, with maybe one day off, then back at it again.

I didn't care. I was happy to have a steady flying job with what is called a "scheduled carrier." It really *was* an airline job, except the planes were smaller, the flights were shorter, and the pay was lower. My career was going places, but I thought I'd make more money at it.

Five days later I showed up at Carlsbad Airport for my first day at work. The big shock came in learning to operate in and out of Los Angeles International Airport (LAX). The commuters were feeders to the big airlines, so most of our flights operated either into or out of there. For a new pilot, it was a madhouse. It seemed you were always running behind or in someone's way – literally on-the-job training. The classroom hadn't prepared me for this. It felt like learning to swim by being thrown into a river of raging rapids. I almost longed to be casually circling over a fire.

The Embraer Bandeirante.

A typical day might go like this. If you were based in Carlsbad, you'd fly one leg to Los Angeles, unload and reload passengers, take a ten-minute flight to Orange County (Santa Ana), return to Los Angeles, go to Santa Barbara, go back to LAX, go off to Palm Springs, go to LAX again, and then finish up where you started at Carlsbad.

We also flew to San Diego, Bakersfield, Ontario, San Luis Obispo, and Santa Maria. It was a "hub and spoke" operation. LAX was our hub and the other airports were our spokes.

Eight legs a day was average, but my logbook shows many days had nine and ten takeoffs and landings. If you were lucky, each takeoff was accompanied by a landing. Flight times were usually seven to eight hours per day, but that was just time in the air. Taxiing and sitting in line waiting to take off or while you were at the gate paid nothing. To get those seven to eight hours of flight time, you might work twelve hours or more a day.

After work, there was just enough time to eat dinner at a fast-food place before you'd drive home, go straight to bed, and get back up at four o'clock in the morning. After eating more fast food on the way to the airport, you'd it all over again.

From where I was staying, it was an hour-and-forty-five-minute drive to Palomar Airport in Carlsbad. Flying out of San Diego would add four hours of driving on top of a twelve- (or more) hour workday.

There was a lot to do in a short amount of time. First, the copilot would preflight the airplane, including a walk-around. The passengers were already on board when the gate agent handed the manifest to you. You manually calculated a weight and balance, which the captain would check and approve (or not). If not, you had to do it again. Next, you had to listen to and write down the ATIS, or automated terminal information service. Some captains helped with these chores, but not all did. Trying to get a word in on the ground control frequency to get your IFR clearance back then was a nightmare.

This was 1983 and LAX still didn't have a designated clearance delivery frequency. It was done on ground control while the same guy was directing airplanes on the taxiways. It wasn't unusual to spend ten minutes or more trying to get a clearance.

Meanwhile, behind the open cockpit door, a planeload of impatient passengers was sitting in a sometimes very hot airplane with little or no air conditioning. Also, an annoyed captain was waiting for you.

After receiving and reading back your IFR clearance, you had to try calling ground control again to get a taxi clearance. While the captain taxied out, you made announcements to the passengers. The FAA didn't require flight attendants on eighteen-passenger airplanes, so one of the pilots had to handle those tasks. You tried to sound cheerful, casual, and friendly and not too busy or rushed.

In almost all multi-crew flight operations, the copilot flies the airplane on every other leg while the other pilot operates the radios and does certain navigation work and checklists. Los Angeles International was a busy environment, but most of these captains did the job with nonchalant ease as if they'd done it a thousand times… which they had, perhaps more. I was amazed at the skill of the captains I flew with.

With short flight times and the repetition of doing everything over and over with no autopilot, it wasn't long before you'd memorized everything: radio frequencies, VOR radials, ILS frequencies and inbound headings, decision heights, tower and ground control frequencies. It was normal to fly all day and never pull out a chart.

In any passenger-carrying job, you must be concerned with the folks in the back: keep them comfortable and informed, try to fly smoothly, and get them where they need to go safely and on time. The air conditioning on the Bandeirante was terrible. If the motors weren't running, there would be none. When they *were* running on the ground, it was inadequate. Anything above eighty degrees was uncomfortable.

In Palm Springs the temperature might be one hundred and ten degrees in the summer. There was an air conditioning cart, but sometimes it didn't work. The wind coming through Banning Pass and the desert thermals made for a turbulent ride in and out of Palm Springs. It was almost always hot and rough. The airsick bags got a lot of use. Many passengers hated the Bandit.

It was hard work but great experience. We worked harder than "real" airline pilots in the big jets and got paid practically nothing by comparison. It was like airline pilot boot camp. If you could survive this, you could survive anything.

Many a dark morning, when the alarm clock went off, my foggy mind toyed with easier ways to make a living, like digging ditches.

It was always long days of short hops and quick turnarounds, often with no chance to eat anything. Getting behind was never our fault, as there were too many outside influences like long lines of airplanes taxiing to the runway or weather delays.

Sometimes you had to delay a flight just to get out and use a bathroom because there were none on the airplane. Frequently a break was written into the schedule, but if you got behind, it evaporated and you just kept going. Some pilots brought lunch boxes or small coolers with them, which was a good idea. I don't know why, but I never did that.

I enjoyed the rare "long" flights to and from San Luis Obispo. It was about an hour each way and radio traffic was low. I'd relax and look out the window at the Pacific Ocean, wondering what it would be like to fly to Hawaii or New York.

I was always careful not to mention my history in the motorcycle club, lack of formal education, and arrest record to anyone in the aviation world. I had no expectations of getting a job with a major airline like United, Delta, or American, but I did want to fly jets!

I especially loved the Learjet, a sleek, sexy hotrod. It had the reputation of being challenging to fly. At that time, it was about as close as you could get to flying a fighter jet in the civilian world.

Setting small goals, I'd worked my way into a job flying small airplanes and training students, then flying the twin-engine Cessna O-2 on the fires.

Now that I'd worked up to turboprop airliners, I started setting my sights higher: a seat in a Lear. If I never got a better pilot job than that, I'd be happy.

If you think it's hard to meet new people,
try picking up the wrong golf ball.

~Jack Lemmon

Chapter 22
LaLa Land

One of the interesting things about flying in and out of Los Angeles International all day is its proximity to Hollywood. Back then, most movie stars and celebrities didn't fly on private jets. They usually flew commercial like everyone else.

Hardly a day went by that you didn't have someone famous on your airplane or see them in the terminal. I never bothered them or asked for an autograph. Normally we had no interaction. They were just passengers to us.

I remember having Andy Williams on board from San Diego to LAX. He was very quiet and reserved. 'Quite an introvert,' I thought at the time.

Ken Norton, the boxer, was polite and friendly. He stuck his head in the cockpit to say hello and shook our hands. His hand was so big, it was like trying to grasp a smoked ham. His weight on the manifest was two hundred and forty pounds. He looked very fit.

The big airlines average the passenger weights under FAR Part 121: one hundred sixty pounds in the summer and one hundred eighty in the winter to allow for extra clothing. Under Part 135, with smaller airplanes, they had to know the exact weights. Many passengers were offended when the gate agent asked how much they weighed.

The gate agents who dealt with celebrities had their own opinions of them. They said the nicest person they ever met was comedian Red Skelton, who was polite and friendly. The gate agents loved him, and he seemed to love them back. It was like he loved everyone. He rode on us a lot going back and forth to his home in Palm Springs, a popular destination for the rich and famous. The worst was a famous comedian, a lady from a long-running sitcom. According to the gate agents, she was an elite snob and treated everyone like servants. Another was a talk show host. I can only take their word for it. As pilots, we rarely had any interaction with them.

One day I was talking to a captain who was a friend of mine. He said earlier that day he'd had Michael Jackson and Diana Ross on his airplane traveling together to San Diego.

One day we picked up Kenny Loggins in Santa Barbara. He took the time to say hi and chatted a little before taking his seat. We were flying to LAX and then on to Palm Springs

After landing he stayed on board while everyone else got off. While boarding the new passengers to Palm Springs, we got a call on the radio from operations to hold for a VIP.

We waited and waited, impatient to keep to our schedule. There were no ground carts to pump cold air into the cabin, and the passengers were hot. Finally, a long black limo arrived and parked at the foot of the stairs next to our airplane.

Out stepped a bodyguard who opened the back door for Henry Kissinger. He and the bodyguard got on board without saying anything to us. Not that they needed to. I wondered if the bodyguard was armed, but back then it wasn't required that they let us know.

When we arrived in Palm Springs, another black limo was waiting for us. As we shut down the engines, it pulled up to the plane. Kissinger and his bodyguard got off first and climbed into the limo, which disappeared across the tarmac.

Before getting off, Kenny Loggins stuck his head in the cockpit again with an amused look on his face. He said, "If I'd have known 'Ol' Hank' would be on this plane, I'd have taken another flight."

I just smiled and shrugged. He flashed that million-dollar smile and walked out the door and down the steps with the rest of the passengers.

In Los Angeles the next day our airplane was taken out of service due to a mechanical problem. I was told to deadhead (ride as a passenger) to what was then my home base in San Diego.

Just before departure I was sitting on the right side near the window, reading a paperback, when someone plopped onto the seat next to me. It was Kenny Loggins.

He said, "Hello again."

"Oh, hi. Did you get invited to Kissinger's dinner party?"

He let out a sharp laugh and rolled his eyes.

I said, "Hey, I really like your work."

The turbine engines started to spin up and it was getting louder, making it difficult to talk. He raised his voice and said, "Thank you very much."

I went back to my book, and he pulled out a newspaper. He was very down-to-earth and humble, just a regular guy. We didn't speak again until after we landed in San Diego, where we said goodbye. He was already a superstar, and not long after that, he performed the title song for *Footloose* and then "Danger Zone" for the movie *Top Gun*.

One day, on a trip from San Diego to Los Angeles, basketball star Larry Bird came on board. He was too tall to sit in a regular seat, so he placed himself in the front aisle seat. After the door was closed and we got moving, he stretched out his long legs into the cockpit between us with his feet crossed. Again, there was no cockpit door on the Bandeirante.

***

Airplanes can always be dangerous, and they don't even have to be in the air for that to be the case. A chilling thing happened one night in San Diego while I was still a copilot. We pulled into a gate on the last leg of the night. We had ferried it back with no passengers. Because it was late, the ground crew wasn't there to guide us in, and we stopped short of our parking spot. We never used jet bridges, just the stairs built into the front door.

Wayne had the left engine shut down, which we did most of the time during taxi operations because it saved fuel. The right engine was still running. While waiting for the ground crew, I heard the whine of jet engines getting closer. Looking to my right, I saw a TWA 727 pulling into the gate next to us. They were really close and had stopped. The captain was looking down with uncertainty. Like with us, there was no ground crew to guide him in.

Unbuckling my harness and hopping out of my seat, I told Wayne, "I'm going to clear the right wing for him." Ducking through the cockpit door, I went back, opened the passenger door, and climbed down the stairs into the moist ocean air of Lindbergh Field.

I hadn't put in any earplugs or hearing protectors, and the engines of the 727 were very loud. Jet engines cause a lot of hearing damage, and after years of riding motorcycles and occasionally shooting guns without ear protection, I already had my fair share of hearing loss.

So, sticking my fingers in my ears, I stepped down onto the ramp and walked around the nose of the Bandeirante. Heading for our right wingtip, I stood and looked up at the captain of the 727. The lights were on in the cockpit, and I could see the pilot's overhead panel. I was mesmerized by the approximately one million gauges and switches.

I was a little distracted as I admired their airplane. Leaving my right ear unprotected, I gave him a thumbs up to let him know he was clear and could pull up to the jet bridge.

He nodded, released his brakes, and pulled the big jet up even with the bridge opening. Then he gave me a thumbs up as a thank you. He left one engine still running as I returned the thumbs up and shoved my finger back in my right ear. I turned on my heel and headed back across the dark ramp toward our airplane. Over the loud whine from the 727 engine, I suddenly heard a new noise. After about six steps I froze in my tracks. Turning my head slowly to my left, I saw a seven-foot-diameter meat cleaver spinning about two feet from my left elbow. I realized Wayne still had the right engine running, and I had paid no attention to the danger.

Having worked about twelve hours that day, I was a bit fatigued and wasn't as alert as I should have been.

Being in front of a propeller is nothing like being behind one. There's little sensation of airflow. Nobody ever walks into a running propeller from the rear. It's always from the side or the front.

Stunned, I foolishly stood there, still with my fingers in my ears for several seconds as I stared in disbelief at the harbinger of death just inches away. My mind slowly started comprehending how careless I'd just been.

I shivered in the warm night air.

Turning back toward the nose of the airplane, I circled to the open doorway, climbed the stairs, and pulled the door shut.

As I sat back down in my seat, the ground crew showed up to guide us in. Setting the parking brake, Wayne told me to shut down the engine. Our day was done.

I was so mortified at my carelessness that I didn't say anything to him about how close I'd just come to a very messy death.

The captain grabbed his flight bag and left to go home. I sat in the now dark, quiet cockpit. An old saying came to mind: "Aviation in itself is not inherently dangerous. But to an even greater degree than the sea, it is terribly unforgiving of any carelessness, incapacity, or neglect."

I think I'd just displayed all three of those.

When it is obvious that the goal cannot be reached,
don't adjust the goal, adjust the actions.

~ Confucius

Chapter 23
Upgrade

By the summer of 1984, because of the deregulation of U.S. airlines and the Reagan economy kicking in, there was finally some movement in the seniority list of pilots at Imperial.

People were getting hired at the big carriers, and copilots were moved up to the left seat to take their place. Most of the captains at Imperial were overqualified to be flying eighteen-passenger turboprops anyway.

In the 1970s and early 1980s, there was a lack of flying jobs, leading to highly qualified pilots working at small commuter airlines. Things were about to change.

In May 1984, after eleven months in the right seat at Imperial Airlines, I was given the chance to upgrade to captain. It was a big honor for me, knowing privately where I'd come from,

There was no real training. For two weeks I flew the line in the left seat with a captain in the right, breaking me in. Because of the steering tiller on the left side, you could taxi the airplane only from the left seat.

Flying regular schedules with passengers on board, there were no simulated engine failures on takeoff or single-engine approaches. As usual, it was all about saving money.

The check ride was tough. I've included the details in the back of this book after the aviation glossary. I hadn't done maneuvers like that since my Citation check ride over a year ago. It was probably the most grueling hour and twelve minutes I'd experienced in any airplane so far.

Whisky Juliet, the Bandeirante I took my check ride in.

I don't know how, but I passed. I was now a Bandeirante captain, having climbed another rung on the ladder of success. I admired most of the captains whom I'd flown with and learned from, and now I was one of them. The work was the same as before, only now I was the boss in charge of the little office in the sky.

Pilots are interesting personalities. That's especially the case with captains, but I was about to find out that copilots are too.

Most captains are the best people you could ever work with. Some, though – not so much. They can let their authority go to their head and confuse responsibility with power. I always thought it was an odd concept to regard being in charge of an airplane as "power." However, I saw it over and over. Egos are funny things.

Ask any pilot who has ever worked in a multi-crew environment and they'll tell you that, now and then, with certain individuals, a little Jekyll and Hyde monster comes out.

It's the same in many offices in the business world: "So-and-so was great until they made him the boss. Now everyone hates him."

An airplane cockpit is no place for personality conflicts, but it happens.

A Chinese proverb says:

"We have no friends and no enemies in life,
only teachers."

I like to shorten that to: "Everyone is a teacher."

As a copilot, I'd already had a lot of teachers – captains to emulate and learn from but also a few others who inadvertently taught me how not to be. Once again, that's life.

I got a whole ten-dollar-an-hour raise for being in the left seat and taking all the responsibility for my passengers' lives. I was now making sixteen dollars and twenty-eight cents an hour. To me, the job was the same, only more relaxed now that I could set the tone in the cockpit.

The EMB 110 Bandeirante was a tough and relatively simple aircraft – very reliable for pilots though not very comfortable for passengers.

I had only one engine failure the whole time I flew it, and that was on final approach to LAX runway 25L. Later, I found out that a compressor bleed valve stuck closed, causing the engine to "compressor stall." After putting down partial landing flaps and the gear, I pushed the throttles back up to maintain approach speed. The right engine started popping and the exhaust gas temperatures, or EGT, went straight to the redline while the engine produced no power.

Crossing over the 405 Freeway, I pulled back the right throttle and advanced the left while shoving in a good bit of left rudder. Leaving the flaps where they were, I flew it to the runway and landed. We didn't have time to notify the tower and we didn't need to as long as we weren't told to "go around."

I told the copilot to shut the engine down as I taxied in on the left side and called it in to the company while he spoke to ground control. That aircraft was done for the day until they could fix it.

Based on only one hundred hours per month, a copilot could expect to make seven thousand five hundred and thirty-six dollars per year. Captains, on the other hand, would make a whopping nineteen thousand five hundred and thirty-six dollars per year. However, nobody flew only one hundred hours per month. It was always more. It wasn't voluntary, as the company scheduled it that way. Some of the pilots were trying to unionize us into ALPA, the Air Line Pilots Association. The company threatened to fire them and anyone who joined the union. We did it anyway, and no one got fired.

My biggest month was one hundred twenty hours, and I knew some guys who flew one-thirty or more. Today, due to the fatigue factor and after numerous accidents, the FAA prohibits that kind of sweatshop labor for FAR Part 135 pilots.

Even with the high-pressure work environment, there were never any accidents or mishaps as far as I'm aware.

Continuous improvement is better than delayed perfection.

~Mark Twain

Chapter 24
There's got to be a better way

In the early 1980s, three things started to turn the aviation world around. First was the Airline Deregulation Act of 1978, which in part caused low-cost startup airlines to pop up all over the country. Second was the Reagan economy starting to kick in. Third but affecting only one airline was the B-scale pay rate at American Airlines.

Captains and even copilots were leaving outfits like Imperial as they got hired by the big carriers. Everyone was excited about who they were applying with. All those months and years of long hours and low wages were about to pay off.

An ATP rating wasn't required, just a commercial-multi-engine-instrument rating. Imperial pilots were perfectly poised to take advantage of the airline expansion. But not me. I didn't even bother to apply because of my background, lack of education, and arrest record. I was convinced no airline would hire me.

On the other side of town in Burbank was an outfit called Devarian Airways, which flew Learjets – sleek, sexy machines with pointed noses. They look like they're wearing wrap-around sunglasses, and they have a T-tail and fuel tanks on the ends of the wings that look like bombs. The Learjet is a handful: small, light, and very powerful. It climbs like a rocket, and an inexperienced pilot can let it get away from him or her. Problems like blasting through assigned altitudes, overshooting final approach headings, and exceeding speed limits in lower airspace happened a lot.

Some of the guys I knew at Imperial had left and gone to work for Devarian. Word was getting around that they needed more pilots.

During the time of the super-high interest rates of the late 1970s and early 1980s, the banks were losing enormous amounts of money on the "float," which was the delay in processing paper checks. The Federal Reserve found they could fly checks written all over the country and deliver them overnight to the big banking centers, mostly in New York City. This was long before electronic banking.

During the late 1970s the Fed and the banks would rent a Learjet, throw on a few bags of checks written that day on the West Coast, and have them in banks in New York the next morning. At that time they paid to fly the jet back to Burbank empty and still made money.

By 1984 Devarian Airways was a fairly big operation with flights not only to New York but all over the country.

They also started carrying small package freight to augment the check business. This was one of the reasons they needed more pilots.

***

It was nine o'clock on a July night when I showed up at Burbank Airport. I turned off Empire Avenue and went through the gate to the ramp at Hangar Four. The night had that typical Southern California thick mist hanging in the air from the frequent marine layer that crept in from the Pacific Ocean.

I parked my car and walked into the hangar to find my buddy Frank, who'd been a captain at Imperial when I was a copilot. He'd been flying for Devarian for a few months, and I was there for a familiarization ride with him in the Beechcraft King Air 200.

Between my experience at Imperial, airline transport rating, and Citation type rating, I was well qualified. They started you out in the King Air flying single pilot. If I proved myself and didn't get lost or crash, I'd work my way up to being a copilot on the Learjet.

The King Air was a T-tailed corporate turboprop with engines that were almost identical to what was on the Bandeirante. Like the rest of the aircraft at Devarian, it was used not for executive transport but for cargo.

Devarian liked to hire Imperial pilots because we had a lot of experience with the Pratt & Whitney PT-6 turboprop engines.

After some small talk Frank and I went to the aircraft to preflight it. Then we waited for the show to start. This would be a familiarization ride and I'd be going with him on regular scheduled runs.

They called it "the sort" and it was quite an operation, perhaps better described as controlled chaos. At 9:50 PM, Learjets, Falcon 10s and 20s, and other King Airs taxied in, parked, and shut down while pickup trucks raced in the gate and helicopters floated down to land. Several fuel trucks were standing by.

On the aircraft, trucks, and helicopters were bags of checks and small package freight. People ran madly in all directions as the cargo was distributed to the right aircraft to go to the right cities. Captains on the jets, however, sat calmly in their cockpits, copying ATIS and getting their pre-filed IFR clearances. The copilots caught the tossed bags of cargo and threw them to the rear of the aircraft.

The King Air pilots flying alone had to do it all themselves: order fuel, help load their airplanes, and get their clearance as they taxied out. It was always "hurry, hurry, hurry!"

When the loading was complete, we were supposed to fasten a cargo net over everything, but nobody took the time to do it. Keeping on schedule was all-important. The King Air had one door at the left rear, and sometimes you had to crawl over the cargo just below the ceiling to get to the cockpit. In case of a crash, if the load slid forward, you'd be trapped and couldn't get out. Nobody thought the cargo net would help anyway.

At precisely 10:00 PM, all the jets and King Airs would fire up, taxi out, and take off in all directions. Frank and I were among them. Once we were in the air, flying off into the dark of night with almost no radio chatter was a pleasure compared to the meat grinder of the Southern California commuter world.

We were on our way to Las Vegas, then Salt Lake City, and finally Denver to spend the next day. I was in the right seat for the first leg. Then, out of Las Vegas, he put me in the driver's seat to get familiar with the airplane.

The bad part was that you were almost always flying at night.

The good part was that you were almost always flying at night.

It was bad because it could be difficult to stay alert in the middle of the night and early morning, depending on your circadian rhythms. It was good because flying with so little traffic was easy, there was no waiting for takeoff or landings, and you often got direct routing wherever you wanted to go. The controllers dealt with you almost every night, so they knew who you were and what you needed.

After the Bandeirante, the King Air was a nice airplane to fly: smoother and quieter. It was similar in size and weight to the Bandit, but the engines were more powerful and the cabin was pressurized. It could cruise higher and faster by almost one hundred knots. With no passengers to think about, the job seemed easy.

As pilots, we didn't have to worry about what cargo went where. The bags were labeled, and there were always ground crews to do that. They worked quickly and efficiently.

The company didn't care about how much gas we used, only that we were on time.

Unlike the Bandeirante, the King Air had an autopilot and was much lighter on the controls. It was a pleasure to fly – more like a Lincoln Town Car as compared to a pickup truck.

Cruising at twenty-five thousand feet on the way to Denver, Frank and I talked about flying for Imperial.

He said, "So you've finally had it flying ten legs a day for ten days in a row?"

"It's not always ten days in a row, but yeah, I've had it. I think I'm getting burned out."

"I still can't believe the time you barrel-rolled that Bandeirante at night. A perfect one G roll. We didn't even lose any altitude."

"Remember, there weren't any passengers. You haven't told anybody about that, have you?"

"Well, yeah, but I didn't say who did it."

"Thanks. I could get in a lot of trouble for that. I guess I spent too much time hanging out with Bob Hoover."

"Wait till you get into the Lears. I've been flying copilot for a couple of weeks now. You're gonna love it."

"I can't wait."

"I don't recommend you rolling it, though."

We both laughed.

After our last leg of the night, the sun was breaking the horizon as we parked the airplane in front of an FBO at Denver Stapleton. We walked to the crew car to drive to the company-owned condo.

Rather than pay for hotel rooms, Devarian Airways had bought condominiums in destination cities all over the country for the pilots to stay in. It was a good investment and saved a lot of money. They were two-bedroom condos, so pilots always had their own rooms.

We drove back and forth in old Mercury Bobcat station wagons that had been purchased from the Coca-Cola company. Dinner/breakfast might have been an Egg McMuffin or a breakfast burrito at a drive-through. We were usually in bed by eight in the morning.

After getting up at four in the afternoon, we made the beds with clean sheets for the next crew, which was required. Then we drove to a restaurant for dinner – or was it breakfast?

Arriving back at the airplane at eight o'clock, we still had an hour before departure. That was plenty of time to preflight the airplane and get our IFR clearance to Salt Lake City.

At nine, two mini-pickups showed up with a small number of bags and boxes. We loaded up and taxied out right on time.

During a brief stop in Salt Lake City, we took on more cargo and gained an hour of time zone as we sped to Burbank, becoming part of the pandemonium of the ten o'clock sort.

Once more, as we parked in front of Hangar Four, helicopters were noisily dropping out of the night sky as pickup trucks raced onto the ramp.

The ground crews were running from vehicles and helicopters to the jets and then back to us. I was throwing bags out the door, then loading more bags for the flight to San Francisco.

At ten o'clock the jets taxied out first because they had the farthest to go. They raced down the runway to haul ass to Dallas and Chicago. Right behind them, we took off, heading northbound. As we got on the departure frequency, the jets were already climbing through ten thousand feet and leaving it to go to the Los Angeles Center frequency as they rocketed for altitude.

I marveled at the speed at which they flew and climbed. I couldn't wait until I could fly them. Besides the French-made Falcon 20s and Falcon 10s, Devarian owned or leased four Lears.

After the frenzy of landing, unloading, loading, and departing, the night became quiet again as we switched to LA Center and had a leisurely flight to SFO.

Upon arriving at the cargo ramp on the north side of the airport, we unloaded our cargo and took on more, fueled up, and turned around to fly back to Burbank, arriving minutes before midnight. The second sort of the night was about to begin. We were just in time to deliver more bags of checks and packages to the Learjet that was flying non-stop to Teterboro, New Jersey.

This sort was smaller and less frenzied. Once our airplane was empty, our work was done for the night. We paused to watch the Lear taxi to the runway, then locked the King Air's door, dropped the logbook off at the office in the hangar, and walked to our cars in the parking lot. Frank and I were finished with my familiarization ride. I drove home for a day off before going back to my current job at Imperial.

This trip gave me a chance to evaluate if I wanted the job, but I already knew I did. I was tentatively hired but had to wait for an opening.

I liked the King Air, and it was nice to fly to multiple states at twenty-five thousand feet instead of short hops at five thousand.

In the meantime, it was back to the salt mines. At least now, in the left seat, I was making more money.

I was based in San Diego, and with the extra pay I was able to share an apartment with my friend Neil Emery. We'd worked together at Sis-Q Flying Service. In addition to being a highly qualified mechanic, he was now working at Imperial as a pilot. As if that wasn't enough, in his spare time, he went to law school.

Our apartment was only ten minutes from the employee parking lot at San Diego's Lindbergh Field. It was great and sure beat the two-hour drive each way to my mother's place in Banning.

Days turned into weeks, then months, flying the same flights over and over. The workhorse Bandeirante remained mostly reliable, with few issues and no emergencies.

The thing with aviation is, more goals always seem to be hanging out in front of you, like that brass ring on a merry-go-round. I was earning my way as a commercial pilot and was content that I'd achieved my goal, but now I had a slot to fly jets at Devarian and couldn't wait for it to open up.

*The moment you stop making mistakes is the
moment you stop learning.*
~Miley Cyrus

Chapter 25
I love it when a plan comes together

In the first week of December I got a call from Mike, the chief pilot at Devarian. There was finally an opening for me. I danced a jig after hanging up the phone. My plans were coming together, and I was moving up in the aviation world.

I gave notice to Imperial that I was leaving, but I still had two more weeks to go.

Devarian wanted to start training me right away. I spent my days – or nights – off flying the King Air on revenue flights while finishing up in the Bandeirante until my time was up. It was beginning to feel like I was in the air more than I was on the ground.

I spent a total of seven nights flying the King Air on revenue flights, with other pilots watching and evaluating me. It was nice to learn the operation and get used to the airplane under normal conditions. There was no real training, nor was there a ground school. I was handed an aircraft manual and told to memorize it.

At the end of the first week, they scheduled me for a check ride. Once again, under a hood with one of their check airmen, we did the usual engine failure on takeoff and single-engine approaches of all kinds into Fox Field and Palmdale. After my captain's check ride at Imperial, it was a piece of cake.

There was no such thing as automation dependency at Imperial. Constantly hand-flying the Bandeirante had prepared me to fly a new airplane while handling simulated emergencies for which I hadn't been trained. Cutting corners to save money was a hallmark of Devarian Airways, as it was with many aviation companies.

Two nights later I showed up and was let loose on my own with a King Air, flying six legs and eight hours from Burbank to Las Vegas, back to Burbank, on to San Francisco, to Burbank again, then to Denver, and finally back to Burbank as the sun came up.

The morning rush hour on the LA freeways was in full swing, and I struggled to stay awake as I drove two hours home to get some sleep and drive back that night to do it all over again. Welcome to my new life… I was happy to be there. It was almost as busy as Imperial, except the flights were longer and quieter and the bags of checks never complained.

Fortunately, most nights weren't that long. It would usually be only three or four legs per night. I spent many days at a condo in Denver, Salt Lake City, or San Francisco, which was nice when I didn't have to make a four-hour round-trip drive.

All the pilots were issued huge key rings, so we had access to crew cars and condos all over the country.

A King Air 200 in flight.

***

One night, Woodrow, another guy I knew from Imperial, was on the San Francisco-Burbank-San Francisco run in a King Air. This is his story as he related it to me.

After arriving at Burbank, he'd have normally gotten gas before heading north again, but he was distracted by talking to a mechanic about his number two comm radio not working.

The mechanic said, "It'll take fifteen minutes to replace it."

Woodrow said, "I don't have time for that. We'll do it tomorrow."

He had to start loading his airplane. Remember that I said the King Air pilots had to do everything themselves.

An hour later he was over the blackness of the bay on a long final approach to runway 28 right at San Francisco. It was eleven-twenty at night and he was descending through five thousand feet fifteen miles from the airport when his left engine quit. His eyes shot to the gauges to see what had happened. Then the other engine quit. Dead silence!

Suddenly a little bell went off in his head and he looked at the fuel gauges next to his left elbow. His heart sank. They both read empty.

He couldn't help but stare at one still propeller and then the other as he realized he was now flying a glider.

With a flood of adrenaline, his mind raced as he hit the mike button and said, "Bay Approach, Devarian eight-victor-golf declaring an emergency. I've lost both engines."

"Eight-victor-golf, Roger, you've lost an engine. Can you continue the approach?"

"Negative, I've lost BOTH engines!"

"Have you tried to restart?"

"I don't think that's going to work."

"Roger that, eight-victor-golf, can you make Palo Alto airport at your ten o'clock and three miles?"

"I'm sure as hell going to try."

"Eight-victor-golf, turn left two-seven-zero and say souls on board and fuel remaining."

"Heading two-seven-zero, one soul on board and, uh… zero fuel remaining."

"Eight-victor-golf, confirm… Did you say zero?"

"Yeah, that's right."

"Eight-victor-golf, Roger, contact Palo Alto Tower on one-one-eight point six. Good luck."

Woodrow's pulse was pounding as he stuck the nose down. With the switch on the yoke, he thumbed in some elevator trim to maintain the best glide speed of one hundred ten knots as he turned left toward the lights of the shoreline. The sound of the whistling wind got quieter as the airplane slowed down.

He watched the altimeter unwind through four thousand feet while his mind whirled, trying to remember the glide ratio of this bird. He was encouraged that the sink rate was only eight hundred feet per minute.

Making a herculean effort to sound calm, he changed the radio frequency, flipped on the landing lights, and said, "Palo Alto Tower, eight-victor-golf, emergency aircraft inbound."

The approach controller had already called the tower at Palo Alto on the landline phone, telling him to expect the inbound emergency.

"Eight-victor-golf, you're in sight, two miles, wind is two-six-zero at five knots, you're cleared to land, runway three-one."

"Runway in sight. Cleared to land three-one."

"Would you like the emergency vehicles?"

"Say runway length?"

"Two thousand four hundred forty-three feet."

"That's awfully short. Yeah, let's roll 'em just in case."

"They're on the way."

Fortunately, the airport was on the edge of the bay, with no homes or industrial areas to fly over to reach it.

A mile from the airport he was still at two thousand feet as he angled toward the end of the runway. At half a mile he was still too high, so he put down the landing gear and some flaps to start slowing. He didn't want to land too long on a twenty-four-hundred-foot strip.

Now with flaps and gear, the airplane came down like a rock, and he started thinking he'd made a big mistake. His instrument scan was a laser focus as he watched the airspeed, altimeter, and vertical speed indicator while constantly shifting his eyes through the windshield to the end of the runway.

Panting with his mouth open, he absentmindedly wondered if he'd pass out from hyperventilation. He tried holding his breath.

Leaving the flaps halfway down at four hundred feet with a sink rate of twelve hundred feet per minute, he eased the nose up and trimmed the elevator to slow to approach speed as he started the forty-degree right turn to line up with the runway.

Everything came together as he touched down and rolled out with plenty of room to spare. Bob Hoover would have been proud, especially because he'd never gotten to practice this maneuver.

Surprisingly the company didn't fire him, but we all felt he should have been given a medal for the exceptional flying skills he exhibited.

After an investigation, the FAA suspended Woodrow's license for thirty days. That wasn't so bad. It could have been a firing squad.

Woodrow later got a job with America West Airlines, which would merge with US Airways, which finally merged with American Airlines.

A mistake is valuable if you can do four things with it: recognize it, admit it, learn from it, forget it.

~ John Wooden

Chapter 26
The snowstorm

I was still not immune from making my own mistakes. It was a bad habit I'd been trying to break.

Two weeks after being cut loose on my own, I arrived over Denver for my last landing of the night.

In the dark cockpit, I peered at the dim instrument panel and dialed the radio frequency for the ATIS. The news wasn't good. Denver Stapleton Airport was reporting the weather to be "zero/zero": zero ceiling, zero visibility. It was late January, and they were getting a heavy snowstorm.

It was five o'clock in the morning. I'd been flying for almost seven hours that night and was ready to call it a day... or a night. But now Stapleton was shut down and no airplanes could land.

The weather wasn't any better where I was cruising along in IFR conditions, with both propeller and airfoil anti-ice on. It wasn't clear how high this storm went.

Pressing the button on the yoke, I spoke into the boom mic: "Denver Approach, Devarian 609 is with you at two-five thousand with information Kilo."

"Devarian 609, Denver Approach, descend to one-two thousand and hold at Hondo, intersection, standard pattern, ten-mile legs. We have no expectation of when the weather will clear. Advise intentions."

"Fuel's okay for now. I'll give it a while in the holding pattern and see what happens."

Finding the intersection of two crossing radials from different VORs, I did a direct entry and watched the DME to start the one-hundred-eighty-degree turn.

Having flown the Bandeirante for the last two years with no autopilot, I wasn't used to the one in the King Air for anything other than straight and level flying. I'd been on this airplane for only two weeks, so to keep my workload down, I clicked it off. This was no time to learn.

I felt more comfortable hand-flying it in the holding pattern, hoping it wouldn't be long before the ceiling and visibility lifted so I could land. A few other aircraft were on the frequency, also in holding patterns. One was a Boeing 727 two thousand feet below me.

Checking my alternate, I saw that it was down too. I didn't want to fly a hundred miles in another direction to land in clearer weather at some other airport. If the company had to pay for a hotel and more gas, they wouldn't be happy. I'd do that if I had to, but right now I had a choice: I could keep holding and wait for the weather to clear enough to land here.

After an hour of droning round and round while staring at the instrument panel, I was getting tired. It had been a long night. I started to worry about gas, thinking this might not clear up until tomorrow. My alternate was still down. Where could I go if I couldn't land soon? How much fuel would it take me to get there?

My tired head was spinning with all this math – distance-time-fuel – while I was still hand-flying in the holding pattern. I had to make a decision soon.

I looked at my charts for a solution, finding ATIS frequencies and listening to each airport's weather to see if it was above landing minimums.

Centennial Airport: No, same as Stapleton.

Rocky Mountain Metropolitan: No, they're down too.

Boulder Municipal: No.

Erie Municipal: No.

Maybe I'd need to divert to Kansas. The Land of Oz… What would Dorothy do?

My mind was overtaxed as I tried to think of where I needed to go and how much gas it would take to get there. I had to think of legal fuel reserves. You're not allowed to land with empty tanks.

Somewhere amid this bad dream of going round and round in the clouds in the dark, dividing my attention between hand flying the King Air in the holding pattern, dialing radios, writing down the weather, and trying to find a suitable nearby airport, the radio came alive.

"Devarian 609, say altitude."

My eyes shot to the altimeter and I replied, "Eleven thousand seven hundred. Sorry, I'll get back to one-two thousand."

The ATC controller calmly replied, "Maintain one-two thousand."

Up to this point, none of the airplanes I'd flown had autopilots. It was new to me. With my self-imposed workload, I'd gotten three hundred feet off my altitude – a cardinal sin in instrument flying. Worse yet, I'd admitted it on the radio.

Ironically, just a couple of minutes later, the approach controller said, "Ceiling is now two hundred overcast, visibility four thousand RVR (runway visual range)."

He cleared the 727 holding below me at ten thousand to start the approach, then cleared me to descend in the holding pattern to ten thousand.

Ten minutes later I was crossing the outer marker on the ILS, still hand-flying the King Air to runway 25L. I broke out of the clouds at two hundred feet and saw the approach lights. It was almost dawn, and the snow-covered runway was pale blue. It looked surreal. The runway hadn't been plowed, but I could see the tracks from the landing gear of two previous flights.

At that time of night, the approach controller was doing triple duty. He was also the tower controller and the ground control. He cleared me to taxi to the FBO we used, but before he let me go, he told me to copy a phone number and asked me to call when I got to a phone.

That's always a bad sign. When ATC gives you a phone number, you know you're in trouble.

After locking the door of the King Air, I grabbed my gear and hustled through the foot-deep snow on the ramp to the FBO. Inside the warm building was a pay phone. I inserted the necessary amount of change. The voice that answered was that of the guy on the radio.

He said, "I have to make a report on that altitude deviation. It's not a big deal, but I'll need your name and certificate number."

After giving him the information, I said, "I'm not in trouble, am I? I was checking the weather for alternates and got off my altitude only a little bit. I was correcting it when you called," I fibbed.

He said, "I'm sure it's nothing. I wouldn't worry about it. Relax and have a good layover."

I think he really meant "lawyer."

I thanked him, hung up, and walked out to the Mercury Bobcat. After brushing snow off the windows, I drove to the condo to sleep for the day. The eastern sky was getting brighter as I left the parking lot. It had been a very long night.

***

That evening I flew two legs back to Burbank to finish my trip. Walking through the hangar, I passed the chief pilot's office. Mike was still there so I stopped in and told him about the incident.

He said, "Why weren't you using the autopilot?"

"I'm not used to autopilots and it didn't seem like a good time to experiment."

"You know, you could have just asked the approach controller what was available to divert to. Put the load on him."

"I didn't think of that. I was trying to be proactive."

"How much was it again?"

"Three hundred feet."

"That's nothing! You didn't admit to it on the radio, did you?"

"Yes, and on the phone on the ground."

Cocking his head with a frown, he said, "Never admit anything to the FAA. They're not your friend."

"I didn't know that. I've never had a problem with them before."

"Well, I doubt they'll do anything. Go enjoy your days off and don't worry about it."

***

A lot of flying jobs require night flying. At Devarian, it was about ninety percent. If you flew during daylight, it was usually because you'd just been flying all night.

Staying awake and alert was always a problem. One captain was constantly falling asleep, sometimes even while on final approach to a runway. There was a joke in the company that the shoulder harnesses were there only to keep his head from hitting the instrument panel when he fell asleep.

There are two kinds of airplanes – those you fly and those that fly you…You must have a distinct understanding at the very start as to who is the boss.

~ Ernest K. Gann

Chapter 27

Dreams come true

Flying the King Air wasn't a bad job, as I enjoyed working alone. I was paying my dues again and biding my time until I could fly the jets.

Ten days after the snowstorm incident and exactly one month after my check ride on the King Air, I was assigned to train new pilots coming in. I was no longer the new guy. My flight instructor rating was still current, though in this environment it wasn't needed. I made sure they knew how to use the autopilot. It would have helped me.

The procedure was to put them in the right seat on the revenue flights and let them see how the job was done. After the first day I'd put them in the left seat and let them fly.

If they did okay after a few days of revenue flights, they'd have to memorize the operating manual, then be given a check ride to qualify for going off on their own.

I was told I'd be working in the King Air for six months, but after only six weeks I was instructed to show up early. It was time for my Learjet checkout.

Once again, there was no ground school. Pete, one of the check pilots, sat with me in the cockpit and explained everything I needed to know to fly in the right seat – which was almost nothing. All the captains in the company could fly these airplanes by themselves, and new copilots were pretty much along for the ride until we got up to speed.

You weren't given a photocopied flight manual to the airplane until you were ready to be a captain. For me, that was a long way off.

After the cockpit familiarization from Pete, I was scheduled for a training flight with Mike, the chief pilot.

Mike was a huge guy with an Italian last name. He stood six-foot-five and probably weighed four hundred pounds. It was hard to believe he could even fit in a Learjet, but he was the nicest guy you could ever work for and he flew that airplane like he'd been doing it all his life.

It was late afternoon and the sun fought to get through the layer of smog to light up the cockpit. We sat in front of Hangar Four on a typical Southern California day in late February.

After another brief on the controls and how to set the pressurization, we fired up those magical jet engines. The right one was always started first because the door was on the left, and sometimes we'd have it open until the last minute to load any late cargo.

Everything was new and exciting. I'd been waiting for this day for years.

Mike walked me through my first engine start. Holding the switch to engage the electric starter motor, I heard a dull clunk. The lights dimmed and a slow humming quickly built up into a whine.

When the N1 compressor gauge reached thirteen percent RPMs, he told me to turn on the fuel. The engine lit off with a dull "poof" and both the fan speed and N1 gauges rose rapidly.

Sometimes a ground crew would be standing by with a fire extinguisher to watch for flames. Most of the time, given that we were operating in the middle of the night, no one was there.

At forty-eight percent RPMs, Mike had me switch the starter switch to GEN for generator to provide electrical power to the airplane. To save weight, the one unit did both jobs.

As the turbine RPM gauge raced upward, we watched the exhaust gas temperature gauge (EGT), looking for a dreaded "hot start." If that happened, you'd immediately snap that thrust lever to OFF while keeping the engine windmilling to blow air through the combustion chamber while hoping there was no fire.

After the battery start, we kept a close eye on the battery temperature gauges. If one or both of them got too hot, they could explode. *That* could ruin your whole day.

I'd been flying turboprops, or "turbine"-powered engines, for almost two years and was thoroughly familiar with the whole concept. During training for my Citation type rating, I'd studied and memorized the operation of jet engines.

With the right engine now running Mike called ground control: "Burbank Ground, Lear Two-Three Victor Golf at Hanger Four with information Zulu. We'd like a VFR departure to the north."

Then, to me: "Okay, let's go. Release the brakes, and don't forget to engage the steering."

The nose wheel steered electronically when you pressed an amber button on the control yoke or locked it in with a white button on the center console. The nose wheel steering, like the rest of the airplane, was very responsive.

If you forgot to press one of these buttons and started the airplane rolling forward while pressing one of the rudder pedals to turn, right or left, the airplane would just go straight. Once you remembered the button, if you still had rudder input, the nose wheel would snap to the direction you were trying to go.

If you were turning right, with the captain in the left seat, the left portion of the windshield right next to his head would slam him in the face – not a good way to start a flight.

It also sometimes happened in reverse, with the guy in the left seat wanting to turn left and giving the guy in the right seat a face full of plexiglass. The cockpit was that small.

Sometimes, from either side, you even did it to yourself. You quickly learned to avoid that.

Before getting to runway 26, Mike started the left engine while I taxied. Once we were rolling down the runway, the powered nose wheel steering would disengage at thirty knots. It was way too sensitive at higher speeds.

He had me make the takeoff from the right seat. The acceleration was amazing. Everything happened so fast. I'd just gotten the power set and was focusing on staying on the centerline when he was already calling out, as if one word, "V-1, Rotate."

It seemed we'd just left the ground. Mike had raised the gear and brought the flaps to eight degrees when he was suddenly telling me to get the nose over and level off as he pulled the throttles back to eighty percent power. We were cleared only to three thousand feet.

As the airspeed hit two hundred knots, he pulled them back even further to sixty percent to maintain the required two-hundred-knot speed limit in the airport traffic area.

There was a saying that, when new on the airplane, we were so far behind it, we were hanging off the tail. That was how I felt.

Learjet model 35 landing

The controls were extremely light and sensitive, and the roll rate was fast, especially if you had fuel in those big tip tanks on the ends of the wings that looked like bombs.

I was overcontrolling it, so Mike said to rest my hands on my knees and fly with my fingertips, not my hands. I did as he told me, and my flying smoothed out.

Soon we were cleared to fourteen thousand five hundred feet. I eased the throttles forward and we rocketed skyward while accelerating to two hundred fifty knots.

I couldn't believe how it handled and climbed. I was flying a jet for the first time since getting my Citation type rating less than two years prior. The Citation felt like a golf cart compared to this thing!

To say it was exhilarating would be an understatement – not just the flying itself, but partly because I'd finally achieved another goal, and it felt like a milestone in my life. I was flying a Learjet *and* getting paid for it.

Climbing out of ten thousand feet, we contacted LA Center, which cleared us direct to Bakersfield. Leveling at fourteen-five, I watched the airspeed indicator in amazement as it smoothly swept past three hundred knots. I kept the autopilot off to get the feel of the airplane.

At fifteen miles out, we started our descent, slowing to the two-hundred-fifty-knot speed limit below ten thousand feet.

Contacting the tower, Mike requested "touch and goes."

Bakersfield Tower responded, "Roger, two-three victor golf, expect right traffic for runway three zero right."

As we descended, I moved the throttles to the power settings that Mike gave me as we were cleared for a long final to 30 Right.

With the landing gear down and the flaps set for landing, I slowed to our one-hundred-twenty-five-knot approach speed.

We had clearance for a touch and go, so as soon as the main wheels rolled onto the concrete runway, Mike moved the flap handle to eight degrees while I pushed the throttles forward to takeoff power.

The little jet instantly responded, and within seconds we were back in the air, pulling the gear up and the throttles back to stay in the pattern.

After a circuit of the pattern and another touch and go, we departed back to the south, climbing steeply for thirteen thousand five hundred feet and a short trip back to Burbank.

I'd finally started to feel like I was catching up with that speedster of an airplane by the time we were on final for a straight-in approach to the south.

Landing on runway 15 for a full stop, I hit the toggle switch on the throttle quadrant to deploy the speed brakes. On this airplane, the thrust reverses worked, but Mike said not to use them because we had so much runway left. Most of the time they didn't work because once the airplane was out of warranty, the company didn't want to pay to maintain them. I guess brake pads were cheaper.

It was my third landing that day and I was now qualified to fly as SIC, second in command, of the Learjet.

Later that evening I launched with Pete to San Francisco for my first revenue flight on the Lear. I was on my way and was now finally a working jet pilot, six and a half years after taking my first flying lesson. People have done it faster, but my unconventional path was getting me where I wanted to go. It had been a fun ride so far.

Learjet model 35.

***

After two days of the Burbank-San Francisco-Portland run, I was starting to feel more comfortable in the airplane.

On the third day I did my first Flight 201, the Burbank to Teterboro, New Jersey run, and we went non-stop. I was flying with another captain,

Larry Snyder, and we made it in four hours and thirteen minutes. I was beginning to enjoy this job a lot more.

A month later, in the whirlwind world of flying checks, I was introduced to the Dassault Falcon 20. Made especially for FedEx, with a big cargo door, it was the original cargo plane that FedEx started with in the early 1970s. One of them now sits in the Smithsonian National Air and Space Museum near Washington D.C. next to an Air France Concorde.

It seems most of the airplanes I've flown are now in museums. Interestingly, under the right wing of the Concorde is Bob Hoover's Shrike Commander, and hanging from the ceiling above it is a Learjet. I never flew the Concorde, though.

Compared to the Learjet, the Falcon 20's cockpit had no frills. It was more like a delivery truck, but it was spacious and felt like a small airliner. There were no tiny micro-switches like in the Lear, and the only way in and out was a small drop-down ladder at the front of the cargo door. It had swept-back wings and leading-edge slats, which, in addition to giving you lower approach speeds, would deploy automatically in high-angle-of-attack situations, like approaching a stall. It was a nice safety feature.

Though slightly bigger than the Lear, the Falcon 20 didn't have as much range or weight-carrying capacity. It had odd French engines with the fan portion of the fan-jet in the rear instead of the front. The engines were old and run out, and we were limited to going no higher than thirty-one thousand feet or cruising faster than Mach .70.

This was the only flying job for which I got paid a salary instead of flight hours. By comparison, after zooming around in Lears, it seemed boring to fly such a slow jet. How quickly we get spoiled.

The day after my copilot checkout (two landings at Bakersfield and one at Burbank), I was off on a typical run in the Falcon 20: Burbank-

Phoenix-Dallas-Atlanta-Charlotte-Raleigh Durham, then layover at one of the company's many condos.

The next night we were back in the air to retrace our steps – or, I should say landings. We ended up at Burbank early in the morning to drive home in rush hour traffic. I'd do that for a whole month, and then it was back to the Learjet.

A FedEx Falcon 20 in the Smithsonian National Air and Space Museum, showing the large cargo door.

To most people, the sky is the limit. To those who love aviation,
the sky is home.

~ Jerry Crawford

Chapter 28
Another day on the job... I mean, night

Tim frowned as he looked across the dark cockpit of the Falcon 20. He looked calm, but I could see the stress on his face.

He said, "That thunderstorm wasn't there when I checked the weather half an hour ago."

That meant it was building fast. This weather was coming in like a freight train. We needed to get out of there.

Sitting on runway 18 Center at Charlotte Airport in North Carolina, we alternated our gaze from the brilliant images of red and yellow on the radar screen to look outside at the flashes of lightning straight ahead.

Tim was probably thinking the same thing I was: 'Maybe we should wait for this thing to pass by…' But waiting an hour or more wasn't an option and hopeful thinking wouldn't work. Hurricane Gloria was on its way, and we needed to get outta Dodge. It was only going to get worse.

The tower knew we were cargo pilots and had no passengers to endanger. Over the radio, he said, "That cell is a mile off the end of the runway, but it's clear to the west. Do you want to give it a try?"

Because of the "left seat authority" agreement with the FAA, it was my leg to fly, so I was in the left seat. Tim was the designated captain, but he still wanted my opinion: "What do you think? Want to give it a try?"

Always up for a challenge and certainly a bit of drama, I said, "Sure. If we start a hard right turn right after takeoff, I think we can get around it."

Tim told the tower, "We're good to go. We'd like to make a right turn after liftoff."

"Devarian One Hundred, cleared for takeoff, runway One-Eight-Center, heading your discretion."

This was a ferry flight. We were empty and making a run for it, trying to escape the hurricane. All the banks would be closed for the next few days anyway, and the company didn't want the airplane exposed to damage.

I released the brakes and ran the throttles to max takeoff power. We started rolling, slowly at first, then faster. I was wishing for the speed of the Learjet.

It was an eerie feeling as we rolled straight toward the storm, like we were flying into the mouth of a fire-breathing dragon. The lightning was getting closer and brighter and the bolts hitting the ground were more numerous as we hurtled toward it. I was beginning to think this was a big mistake. When Tim called out, "Rotate," I pulled the nose up while at the same time cranking in a lot of right aileron along with some right rudder. I was lucky I didn't drag the right wingtip.

A bolt of lightning hit the end of the runway, turning the cockpit to daylight, right where we'd have been. I thought, 'That's a lot closer than a mile.' As the gear came up, simultaneous with the flash, we heard the crashing thunder over the whine of the engines as we were in a thirty-degree right bank at low altitude. Another bolt of lightning struck the ground just off our right wing, again nearly blinding us. We felt like we were being shot at. Happily, they were missing.

It was thrilling, an incredible light show, and my adrenaline was pumping. If we'd known more about the dangers of microbursts and windshear, we probably wouldn't have done it. However, we were cargo pilots and hadn't been trained in those kinds of conditions. We were fearless, we were foolish, we were lucky, and we survived.

As we climbed out to the west, Tim said, "Let's not ever do that again."

I said, "I'm with you on that."

***

At some point, Devarian Airways changed its name to Bancjet Systems, but for a long time we still used the Devarian callsign on the radio. Some of the Falcon 20s got a new paint job but not the Lears or King Airs.

One of Devarian's Falcon 20s with the new Bancjet paint job.

Soon I was checked out in the Falcon 10. It was easier to fly and faster than the Lear but not as pretty. We called it our Millennium Falcon.

The engines were Garrett Air Research TFE 731s like in the Lear 35. The cargo capacity was about the same, but it carried less fuel, so it had a shorter range and we rarely flew it east of Chicago or Dallas. It really was a nice little airplane. The trailing link landing gear made it hard to make a bad landing. The wing, which was more swept, like the Falcon 20, had leading edge slats, just like the big jets. This improved lower-speed maneuvering.

We had crews based in Salt Lake City that flew the Falcon 10 all the time. They had a route that went SLC-BUR-MDW-SLC every night. MDW was Midway Airport in Chicago. They were back home every morning, so it was a good place to be based.

There was another route out of Burbank that went to Phoenix, Dallas, Albuquerque, and Burbank – not a bad run for the night. However, I preferred to layover somewhere so I wouldn't have to drive two hours home in the morning, then be back at Burbank that night.

When I got a copilot checkout in the 10 again, it was up to Bakersfield for two touch and goes, then back to Burbank for a third. I was now qualified to be second in command of a third jet.

On my first revenue flight in the little 10, I was paired with Steve Drake, a tall, friendly guy who laughed easily and was a great pilot.

After takeoff from Burbank, we climbed out over the San Angeles Mountains, heading for Chicago. In our hurried departure, we'd left the cockpit dome light on.

Steve was flying. He told me, "Turn out that light, would ya?"

I craned my neck back, trying to see a switch. No luck. So, I unsnapped my shoulder harness/seatbelt and got up for a closer look.

While I was fumbling around, Steve frowned at me and asked, "What's taking so long? How much time do you have on this thing anyway?"

I said, "About thirty minutes. How about you?"

He burst out laughing and said, "An hour!"

I laughed too. We thought it was the funniest thing ever. I finally found the switch, turned the dome light out, and got back into my seat as we sped upward into the darkness. The lack of training from Devarian was becoming legendary.

I believe the skill of those pilots was the only thing that kept the company out of trouble.

***

Just when I thought they'd forgotten about it, I got a letter in the mail from the FAA. It said they were going to suspend my pilot's license for thirty days for the altitude violation over Denver. I didn't want to spend a whole month without pay, so I hired an aviation lawyer to fight it.

After I spent hundreds of dollars, he told me, "There's nothing I can do. You admitted getting off your altitude on the radio and on the phone. The best I've been able to do is get your suspension down to seven days."

When I reported that to Mike, my chief pilot, he said, "Don't worry about it. When they suspend your license for a week, we'll give you a paid vacation."

Problem solved for now, but I felt like a failure. The company didn't seem to care, but not having a clean record could affect any future hiring.

IF you can dream it, you can do it.

~Walt Disney

Chapter 29
Living the dream

Flying the ILS through the snowstorm at one thousand feet above the ground, we crossed the outer marker.

Paul, the captain, kept the ILS needles perfectly centered as he called out, "Gear down, full flaps." I pulled the tiny selector into the down detent and heard the satisfying clunk as the landing gear locked into place. Then I moved the flap lever into the landing position.

Calling out, "Three green, flaps forty," I ran through the final landing checklist.

Large snowflakes hit the wrap-around windshield of our Learjet as we rocketed through the murk. It was like we were flying through a feather pillow. Visibility was zero.

Engine and wing anti-ice were on full as I called off the altitudes on the altimeter. The tower was closed and there had been no braking action reports.

Paul said, "If it doesn't look like we'll be able to stop, I'll get the speed brakes and the throttles. You put the flaps to eight degrees and we'll get the hell out of here."

At two hundred feet above the ground, category three minimums, I called, "Decision height," as the white film engulfing the windshield cleared. We saw the soft blue dawn caressing the snowscape just south of Pittsburgh.

Runway 28 at Allegheny County Airport came into view dead ahead. It was solid white, as was everything, but we could see the outline of runway lights.

No snowplows had disturbed it, and no other airplanes had been on it all night.

We were both tense as our sleek aircraft hurtled toward the ground. Landing this hotrod Learjet on a snow-covered runway with no braking action reports was taking a big risk.

If we couldn't get it stopped, we'd run off the end and crash. Luckily, we had no passengers, so we were risking only our own lives. The boxes and canceled checks in the back of the airplane didn't give a hoot about whether we'd make it.

In seconds we were over the landing threshold. Paul started the flare, easing the throttles to idle and raising the nose ever so slightly.

He made a firm touchdown to drive the main wheels through the snow. When he pulled the toggle switch that activated the speed brakes on the wings, the nose wheel lowered onto the runway. He stomped on both brake pedals.

Nothing! My heart leaped into my throat.

Instead of the expected sudden deceleration throwing you against the shoulder harness, there was no slowing at all. Indeed, it seemed like the airplane accelerated.

It felt like we were sliding on a layer of ice underneath the snow. There was no way we could stop on that runway.

Our thrust reversers were inoperative. The warranty had expired, and the company thought we didn't need them.

Still traveling over one hundred and twenty miles per hour, we saw the end of the runway approaching fast.

Snapping the toggle switch to close the speed brakes, Paul announced, "Okay, let's get outta here. Flaps to takeoff position."

As I ran the lever to the flaps' eight position, he shoved both throttles up to full power. Our speed increased and the end of the runway came at us even faster.

Watching the airspeed indicator, I called, "V-1, rotate," and he lifted the nose. The little jet leaped back into the sky just as the end of the runway flashed beneath us.

Paul calmly said, "Leave the gear out for a minute. They're probably packed with snow. Maybe we can blow some of it off before we put them in the wells."

The white world of zero visibility swallowed us again as he went back on instruments.

Picking up the microphone, I said, "Pittsburgh, Lear One Three Victor Golf is back with you off of Allegheny County. We'd like to proceed to Newark."

Pittsburgh Approach said, "That was quick. Lear Thirteen Victor Golf, turn heading zero eight zero, direct Newark when able, climb and maintain two zero thousand and contact New York Center. Before you go, how was the braking action?"

I repeated the instructions, then said, "Braking action was nil. Thirteen Victor Golf, adios."

Breathing a sigh of relief, I brought up the landing gear and started tuning the comm and navigation radios. Another close call in the risky world of flying canceled checks. There would be more over the years.

***

On Flight 201 the bags of checks were heading to the banking capitals in New York City. When possible, we'd go non-stop, which sounds quicker, but it seemed long and boring because, to stretch the gas, we flew slower at long-range cruise (LRC).

The captains took pride in trying to make the fastest time, and the four-thirteen I did wasn't it. Someone had actually done it in just under four hours – possibly a record unless you were an SR-71.

Part of the non-stop requirement was to have good weather at the destination. If it was overcast you needed to have legal fuel IFR reserves, and it might not work. You also had to have good tailwinds. If not, we'd go at max Mach and land at either Salina, Kansas, or Chicago's Midway Airport for fuel. It was almost like a pit stop for a race car except they didn't change the tires.

Salina was an old Strategic Air Command base made for heavily loaded B-52 bombers. At twelve thousand three hundred feet, it was, at that time, one of the longest runways in the country. Dropping in there in the middle of the night and getting back out was a piece of cake. There were never any delays. We'd call on the radio to let them know we were coming.

Flower Aviation was the FBO there, and it was open all night. When you bought a certain amount of gas, they'd give each of the pilots a bottle of wine and a frozen steak sealed in plastic wrap.

The fuel truck would be waiting for us. As the fueler went to work, we'd bail out of the cockpit and head straight for the lobby and the restrooms.

We'd grab a cup of coffee on our way out, and by the time we got back, the airplane would be full of gas. One of us would sign the receipt, collect our free goodies, and then secure the door while the other guy was firing up the engines. Within minutes we'd be rocketing upward, racing once more to Teterboro Airport.

We preferred Salina because of the long runway and ease of getting in and out. However, when Vic, the owner of our company, found out about the free steaks and wine, he demanded that they be turned over to him. We found reasons not to go into Salina anymore.

The other option was to land at Midway. In the middle of the night, the normally busy airspace around Chicago wasn't a problem. The downside was that the longest runway was only sixty-five hundred feet and the little airport was surrounded by buildings. It was like trying to drop into a small hole with an airport in it.

The routine on the ground was the same as at Salina, just without the free stuff.

Flight times on those nights were usually five to five and a half hours, depending on the winds. Either way, by 8:30 East Coast time, Devarian Flight 201 would be landing at Teterboro Airport on the east side of the Hudson River. In addition to a few small pickup trucks, there would be an Aerospatiale A-Star helicopter waiting with the rotors turning and the pilot at the controls.

Before the airplane came to a stop, the pilot flying would shut down the left engine, and the other one would have the door open. As soon as we stopped, the copilot would start throwing bags onto the ramp. Some would be caught by the ground crews, who would run to the helicopter and throw them through the open door. When it had a full load, the helicopter would lift off and fly across the Hudson River, directly toward the tall buildings of New York City.

Ten minutes later it would land on the World Trade Center dock. More ground crews would frantically load bags into trucks that would race to the various banks in downtown Manhattan. Millions of dollars of checks that had been written yesterday on the West Coast would be at the banking headquarters by nine o'clock in the morning. That was a typical night on Devarian Flight 201.

The pilots would spend the day in the condo in Englewood, New Jersey and try to get some sleep. Waking in the afternoon, we'd do the bed-making routine, then drive to our favorite Italian restaurant for dinner… or breakfast. By eight o'clock we'd be back at the airplane in plenty of time to leave Teterboro at ten o'clock at night. Then it was off to Atlanta, Dallas, Phoenix, and, finally, Burbank.

If you were lucky, you got to go home, but sometimes extra legs would be on. However, I didn't care. Sometimes I needed to pinch myself to make sure I wasn't dreaming.

Or to make sure I hadn't fallen asleep.

Chapter 30
My kingdom for a thrust reverser

One evening I was flying copilot with John, whose nickname was Steak Knife or just Steak for short. He'd gotten that handle because of an altercation in a restaurant one evening on a layover. You might think I was talking about some biker, but no, he wasn't one.

John was one of the most experienced pilots in the company, and I had flown with him many times. This night we were doing the run to Reno and back. He'd fly the first leg.

Sitting in front of the company headquarters at Hangar Four were two beautiful, sleek Learjets. We climbed into one of them, which was empty for the first leg. The plane was fueled up and ready to go, so we closed the door and started our preflight checks. These always seemed rushed and abbreviated due to our normally tight schedules.

Moments later, as we were rolling for takeoff on runway 08 at Burbank, the right engine started surging. With the throttles at full power, the RPMs on the right side rolled back to about sixty percent, then back up to one hundred percent, and then back down again, back and forth.

After a couple of seconds of this, John snapped back the throttles to idle, hit the brakes, and said, "Tell the tower we're aborting." Even without working thrust reversers, five thousand eight hundred feet of runway and an empty Learjet, we stopped in plenty of time.

Turning off onto the parallel taxiway, he said, "Tell 'em we want to go back for another try."

Into the microphone, I said, "Tower Lear Six Six Six Charlie Charlie, we had a little engine issue that time. We'd like to taxi back for another takeoff."

"Roger, Six Charlie Charlie, taxi to runway zero eight. Let me know when you're ready."

Trying to remember the speed at which we aborted, I turned to John and asked, "Do you want me to get out the brake cooling chart?"

"Naw, don't worry about it. It'll be fine."

I should have looked it up anyway, but he was already taxing fast back to the end of 08.

I said, "Maybe we should use runway 33. It's longer and it doesn't have a wall at the end."

"No, we'll be fine."

I was thinking about brake-fade. When brakes get hot, they don't work as well. When they get hot enough, they don't work at all. Think of runaway truck ramps.

The brake cooling chart in the operating manual showed: "If you abort at this speed and you weigh this much, you need this much time to cool the brakes to be safe for another takeoff.'

It was late in the evening and there was no other traffic. When we arrived back at the departure end of the runway, the tower cleared us to go.

We swung back onto the runway, and John stood the throttles up to takeoff power. We were once again thrown back in our seats as the little jet rocketed forward.

All looked good until about one hundred and ten knots when the surging started again. He let it continue for several seconds, hoping it would stop, but it didn't.

Our acceleration slowed and, at one hundred twenty knots, John slammed the throttles to idle. Again, he stomped on the brakes.

We were initially thrown forward into our shoulder harnesses as the airplane slowed, but it seemed we were still going way too fast.

John was standing on the brakes as hard as he could. I'm sure my eyes were getting bigger as we watched the wall at the end of the runway speeding toward us.

I put my hand on the drag chute handle and asked, "Do you want me to pull the chute?"

Steak said, "No, we'll be fine."

He didn't sound as confident this time, and I was getting a little tired of hearing that. I knew the company didn't like us to use the drag chute because it cost them money to repack it.

Glancing over, I saw John's eyes getting big also. I thought I saw sweat breaking out on his face as he stared at the approaching wall, still braking as hard as he could. We were slowing but not quickly. I found myself wishing those thrust reversers were working.

On the other side of that wall was six-lane-wide North Hollywood Way and a gas station – no place for an out-of-control jet. The wall might stop a Learjet, but I sure didn't want to find out.

Finally crossing the very end of the runway onto the overrun, we were almost within rock-throwing distance of the wall when we'd slowed enough to turn onto the taxiway.

Without asking him, I told the tower, "Six Charlie Charlie would like to taxi to Hangar Four."

Cleared by the tower, we headed back to the company headquarters. John said, "Tell the company we'll need that other jet."

They said it was ready to go. Pulling in next to it, he parked the brakes. Checking the EGTs, he shut down the engines and then the batteries.

After opening the clamshell door, I stepped out with my flight bag. John came out behind me. We marched across the ramp toward the other Learjet. We hadn't gotten thirty feet when we heard a loud hissing that sounded like a very angry snake.

Stopping and turning to look, we saw our airplane sinking to the asphalt on flat tires. The fuse plugs had blown.

This is the reason aircraft tires are made with fuse plugs that will melt at extreme heat. Otherwise, without that release, the tires can get hot enough to explode.

If the large tires on a big jet airliner blow up, they could kill anybody nearby – like firefighters who might be there hosing down hot brakes, which can catch fire or might already be on fire.

Neither one of us said anything as we turned back toward the spare airplane. We jumped in and uneventfully completed the run for the night.

I never forgot that lesson: The brake cooling charts are there for a reason. Bigger, more modern airplanes have brake temperature gauges. Sometimes you need to be more proactive with a captain who isn't thinking about what could happen. He just wanted to get the job done for the company – mission-oriented.

We got lucky, but just barely.

A little aside about that runway. On March 5, 2000, Southwest Airlines Flight 1455 landed long and fast on a wet runway 08 and couldn't stop. They went through the blast fence and the wall, crossing Hollywood Way, hitting a car, and coming to rest against the sign of a Chevron gas station.

Surprisingly no one was killed, not even the people in the car, which was stuck under the fuselage of the Boeing 737.

If that had been us, I'm afraid our little Learjet would have been plastered against the wall like Wile E. Coyote chasing the Road Runner.

March 5, 2000.

***

In July of 1985 I'd just been granted "left seat authority" in the Learjet. That meant, when you flew your leg, you did it from the left seat, like the pilot in command. It was a good idea and allowed the copilots to get used to flying in the captain's seat until they got their type rating.

The next evening, after finishing a three-day trip in the Learjet with ten legs, I flew one last leg from San Francisco to Burbank. I expected to go home for an anticipated four days off, but the company had other ideas. On taxi-in, they called and said I needed to come to the office after we parked the aircraft.

The chief pilot told me I'd volunteered to fly to Fresno in a King Air to pick up the owner of the company, Vic Devarian, and his lawyer and bring them back to Burbank. Vic, quite the entrepreneur, also owned a construction company and they had a big job going in Fresno.

Still being current in the King Air, I'd been tagged to fly some revenue runs a few times. I didn't mind because it was nice to fly alone again and was a chance to log some PIC time.

Mike said, "You can take 5 Victor Golf. Oh, and by the way, the autopilot is inoperative."

I hadn't flown the King Air for almost three months, but according to Federal Aviation Regulations, if you'd made at least three landings in ninety days, you were still qualified. So, I collected the keys and the logbook for 5VG, filed an IFR flight plan, and walked out to the dark ramp to find the airplane.

At first, she seemed like a long-lost girlfriend, but my head was filled with my new love: the Learjet. It all came back to me as I buckled in and turned on the battery. The electronic instruments came alive as the gyros started their slow, exciting, winding-up sound.

The flight to Fresno was uneventful, and having no autopilot gave me something to do on the short fifty-four-minute trip. I found Vic and his lawyer as I taxied up to the FBO. It was less than three years since I'd flown in and out of this airport in my O2 working on the fires, but it seemed like another lifetime.

To make room for cargo, there were normally no seats in the cabin. At times, they'd be stacked to the ceiling, but a mechanic had installed a seat for the lawyer.

Opening the entry door behind the left wing, I greeted the two men as they climbed aboard. After securing the door, I headed back to the cockpit. To my surprise, I found the boss sitting in the left seat.

He turned to me and said, "You don't mind if I fly, do you?"

He had a commercial license, and I knew from other pilots in the company who had flown with him that he wasn't very good. Flying skills are perishable, and most commercial pilots fly almost every day. It's easy to get rusty when you don't.

But it was his company and his airplane. What could I say? So I said, "Not at all," as I climbed into the right seat. It had full controls and instruments on the right side and, after all, I still had my flight instructor ratings and had already spent a fair amount of time there breaking in newly hired pilots.

I said, "Would you like me to work the radios?"

"Yeah, I'd appreciate it. I just want to keep my hand in. I don't get a chance to fly much nowadays."

"No problem, I can use a break. By the way, the autopilot is inop, so this will be good practice for you."

He just said, "Oh!"

Of course, it wasn't a break. I had to keep a pretty close eye on him. No matter who owned the airplane, I was still the designated PIC and we were on an IFR flight plan, so I was responsible for everything. If he got off his altitude, it would be my fault.

I had to admit, for someone who wasn't a line pilot, he did a fair job at keeping us on altitude and tracking VOR radials. He even made a passable landing.

Back in Burbank, once the King Air was shut down, Vic said, "I'm worn out. Do you have to do this much, fly with no autopilot?"

I chuckled to myself at the fact that he'd flown only one hour. "Of course," I said. "Sometimes we do it all the way to Teterboro and back." I didn't mention what it was like to hand-fly a Lear in the thin air at forty-five thousand feet. It was a lot harder than buzzing along at twenty-five thousand in a King Air

At a relatively slow long-range cruise speed, operating near the "coffin corner," just between a stall and a Mach overspeed, it was more like trying to balance on top of a bowling ball.

At high altitude, the normally nimble and responsive Learjet was sluggish and wallowed around. It took your full attention. When that happened, we'd usually switch off: One pilot would fly for an hour, then the other one would take over. It was tedious work, which is why they invented autopilots in the first place.

I hoped this little workout would make Vic more conscious of the need to spend money on maintenance for unimportant things like autopilots. I never saw any improvement, though. It was still not unusual to fly an aircraft, even to Chicago or New York, with no autopilot.

Success is getting what you want,
happiness is wanting what you get.

~W.P. Kinsella

Chapter 31
Learjet captain

One September evening after I'd been in the Lear for seven months, Jim Finely and I spent the day laying over at the condo in Salt Lake City.

He was one of those guys you felt like you'd known forever. We'd previously flown together at Imperial Airlines, and he'd already been with Devarian for a year.

Besides working as a pilot, he did part-time bartending. He was tall, dark, and handsome, with an Errol Flynn mustache. Given his easy, friendly manner and great sense of humor, the ladies loved him.

Having dinner at our usual haunt, the Market Street Grill in downtown Salt Lake City, Jim said, "You should be checking out as captain soon. Has anyone given you any training: V-1 cuts, engine out approaches, that kind of thing?"

"No. I'm hoping they will soon, but I haven't heard anything."

"I'll call the office and see if they'll approve a little extra flight time tonight."

"That would be great. I haven't even been given an operating manual yet."

We hurried to finish our freshly caught salmon dinners and then drove to the airport earlier than normal.

The flight office approved the flight time, so before our scheduled departure time and the arrival of our minimal cargo, we fired up Lear N23VG and taxied out. We called ground control, telling them we'd like to do some practice approaches.

On takeoff, Jim pulled back the left engine to idle, simulating an engine failure at V-1, the takeoff decision speed: go or no-go. It was a risky maneuver in a real airplane and the first time I'd experienced it in a jet since I'd flown the Citation two years prior. The Lear was much more of a handful. In that configuration, it fought to kill you, so you had to fight back.

If you messed it up badly enough, and the other pilot couldn't correct it, you could crash. Training accidents like that happened all too often before the advent of simulators. However, Devarian wouldn't pay for simulator training. Why use simulators when we had the real thing?

For the next hour and a half, I wrestled with the airplane in the night as we did engine-out VOR and ILS approaches and full-stop landings. Then we'd taxi back again for another takeoff, where I'd get another engine cut at V-1.

It was hard work, but it was also the first real training I'd had in the Lear that would prepare me for a check ride. Flying a multi-engine airplane on one engine requires constant rudder control and trimming when the power and speed are increased or decreased. In an approach environment, it seems you're always speeding up, slowing down, climbing, descending, or turning.

Back on the ground at our regular departure time, we loaded our cargo of canceled checks from the Salt Lake City banks and raced to Burbank.

Two weeks later I was given another hour and a half of training with Pete in Salt Lake City before the same scheduled run.

Almost two months later, in November, I was tossed an operating manual and told to prepare for my check ride the next week.

I had to study it to memorize systems: electrical, hydraulic, pressurization, fuel, engines, limitations, V-speeds, and everything involved with operating the airplane. You suddenly had to be an expert. However, I'd been flying it for a while, so I was.

The check ride at the end of November was uneventful. Chief Pilot Mike Calabrese sat in the right seat as the FAA check airman watched over our shoulders as we droned around the Los Angeles basin.

Flying by instruments under a plastic hood, I struggled with the airplane for two and a half hours. Operating almost entirely on one engine, I successfully performed V-1 engine cuts on takeoff, then made single-engine approaches into the Long Beach and Santa Monica airports.

After two landings, Jack, the check airman, declared me good to go. We asked for clearance back to Burbank, and I even got to fly without the hood and with both engines running for that short trip. I was elated. I had graduated and life was good.

Descending onto the runway at Burbank, I was walking on air, literally as well as metaphorically. Now, as a qualified captain on the Learjet, I felt as successful as I ever had in my life.

***

Pilots who've flown all night know staying awake can be a problem. Some have a harder time sleeping during the day and being alert at night than others. One pilot was notorious for falling asleep, sometimes on the final approach to a runway. We joked that the only reason the shoulder harnesses were there was to keep his face from hitting the instrument panel when he nodded off.

It was an endurance thing, especially on a Teterboro non-stop. As we climbed out of Burbank, LA Center would clear us direct to Slate Run, a VORTAC and arrival fix near the tiny town in central Pennsylvania. There was little to do except keep an eye on the fuel, change radio frequencies from time to time, and monitor the weather.

Conversation was a good way to stay awake, but often that would lag or some people just didn't have anything to say. It wasn't unusual to suddenly wake with a start, realizing you'd fallen asleep. Embarrassed that you'd allowed yourself to drift off, you'd peek across the cockpit to see if you'd been caught, only to find the other pilot with his eyes closed also.

You'd been hurtling along at six hundred miles per hour with both pilots sound asleep. Not good. You could get into a Mach over-speed situation known as Mach Tuck, which could ruin your whole day.

When that happened, I wouldn't say anything. Instead, I'd double down on my efforts to stay awake and let the other guy sleep. It was certainly better to be napping up at altitude and get some rest than to be falling asleep on approach to the airport.

But please, only one pilot at a time. Believe it or not, some countries have a program allowing for that. It's called CRIP, for controlled rest in position. It's not allowed in the United States, though.

For the airlines, on long-haul international flights, if the flight time is scheduled to be over nine hours, the FAA requires an extra pilot to spell the other pilots, allowing them to get some rest. If the scheduled leg is over twelve hours, two extra pilots must be part of the crew. Fatigue is a constant problem in aviation.

***

We flew four nights a week, from Monday night to Thursday night. Our route network took us all over the country, with crews spending a weekend in different cities every three or four weeks. The airplane would arrive on Friday morning and not leave until Monday night. The pilots did too.

Hanging out in Raleigh, North Carolina or Salt Lake City was a nice quiet getaway, relaxing while watching television or reading a book.

My favorite weekend was staying at the condo in Englewood, New Jersey. We could jump in the indestructible Bobcat crew car and, after a quick trip across the George Washington Bridge, be in New York City in no time – depending on the traffic, of course.

My parents had lived there until the 1940s, and I was curious to see it, having been there only once, when I was a kid.

I've always compared New York City to the zoo: a fascinating place to visit, but I wouldn't want to live there.

Once in the city, it's easier to park the car *if* you can find a spot and use the subway to get around. It cost hardly anything, at least back then. There are so many things to see there that if you're bored, it's entirely your own fault.

Walking the streets, you look up at the enormous skyscrapers from down in the endless valleys of concrete. It's like having vertical cliffs all around – a feeling you get in only a few cities in the world, like Hong Kong, Tokyo, or Beijing.

Restaurants, diners, delis, bars, and bodegas are everywhere, or maybe you just get a hotdog from a street vendor. You can always find someplace to eat or drink twenty-four hours a day. And, believe it or not, most New Yorkers are friendly. The ones who aren't might be tourists.

Central Park is huge, and you can spend all day there. It's a surprising oasis of greenery and bliss in the land of concrete. On Central Park West is one of my favorite places, the Museum of Natural History, which I saw when I was six years old. I went there several times during our long weekend layovers. It contains bones of dinosaurs and dioramas of African animals taken by Carl Akley and Teddy Roosevelt. To me, when I was a kid, it was a magical feeling to experience exotic animals in their natural habitat.

On the streets of New York, it wasn't unusual to walk along the sidewalk and be accosted by mentally ill people who'd yell at you for only reasons they knew, swearing and calling you names. The best thing to do was to keep walking and ignore them. They might have followed you only so far, then started up with someone else, who'd also ignore them.

One incident that happened in the subway always stuck in my mind. I was walking along with Allen, my copilot and friend, a former Imperial guy who'd never been to New York before.

We were in the busy connector under Union Square, going from the Broadway line to the Park Avenue line. There were six different directions of subway cars and thousands of people transferring from one line to another.

You might think, in America, people would stay to the right, like we drive, but that's not what they do in New York. Masses of subway riders flowed in both directions like two herds of wildebeests merging through each other with no order at all. You had to be light on your feet to avoid constant head-on collisions. It was good practice for dancing.

It was wintertime, and down in those tunnels, I felt hot in my trench coat among the throngs of equally bundled-up people. Up on the street, it was biting cold as the wind swept through the concrete canyons.

Ahead and to the left I noticed an individual off to the side, leaning against the wall. He was huge, standing head and shoulders above the crowd. At first, I thought he must be standing on a box. He was raggedy and disheveled, with a beard, and looked homeless.

For some reason, he took offense to someone passing him in the crowd. I couldn't tell who it was. Suddenly this giant came off the wall and began wading into the crowd, yelling at the top of his lungs as he started after someone who was apparently coming in our direction. He hadn't been on a box.

Adept New Yorkers parted like the Red Sea to let him through. Cursing at his target in some kind of guttural street language, he was saying something like, "Hey, you, come back here. I'm gonna kick your ass. Yeah, you, come back here. I'm gonna get you, you m*****f*****…"

I tried to spot who he was after and didn't see any likely suspects, and nobody seemed to be running from him. I turned my head as Allen said, "What's his problem?" I shrugged.

That was my mistake: I took my eyes off the guy. Before I knew it, he was directly in front of me. I tried to stop, and we did one of those little dances where you're both trying to avoid a collision. However, he was moving too fast and slammed right into me.

He was solid as a rock. I bounced off his chest and started falling backward. He reached out and grabbed me by the shoulders, preventing me from falling. He literally picked me up, as my feet left the floor for a moment.

I thought, 'This is it. This guy is going to kill me. Maybe Allen will notify my next of kin and tell them what happened.'

Then, still holding me off the floor, he gently put me upright on my feet and, in a soft voice in perfect English, said, "Oh, excuse me, sir."

He nimbly stepped around me and charged off into the crowd, continuing his tirade, yelling and swearing at the top of his lungs like an angry bull elephant, chasing his possibly imaginary quarry.

I looked to my right. Allen was standing there with his mouth hanging open. Mine probably was too. We were stunned, wondering what had just happened.

As the guy and his booming voice melted away into the crowd, no one else seemed to pay attention to anything other than the fact that we were now in their way. We turned and resumed our flow with the crowd, heading for the Park Avenue line.

Why was he so agitated? Who was he after? Why was he so polite when he crashed into me? Was it just an act? Was he an undercover cop trying to pretend to be something for who knows what reason? It was a strange situation, and I'll never know why it happened.

Allen asked, "What the hell was that all about?"

I just said, "That's New York for you."

New York ,New York
~Frank Sinatra

Chapter 32
Business as usual

As a Lear captain, I worked a route that went from Burbank to San Francisco to Portland to Seattle's Boeing Field, and then over to PSC, which is Tri-Cities Airport at Pasco, Washington.

It also served the neighboring cities of Kennewick and Richland. We'd layover there but no condos. We'd get a day's sleep at a motel before flying back out that night.

Sixteen years earlier I'd spent time in that area, wandering from town to town on my chopped Harley. I was nineteen and I'd had a sweet interlude there for a couple of months with a girl I'd met in my travels. It didn't last because I had to move on. The call of the road was too strong. I wrote about it in my first book, *Hangmen*.

I'd been a homeless biker running from the law, with no money, no job, and no ambitions. What would she think of me now? Would she be proud of me?

It was small-town America, and it seemed like a lifetime ago. Looking through the phone book in my motel room, I couldn't find her. Had she married and changed her name? Had she moved away? I'd been working all night. Now I needed to get some sleep and be ready to fly that evening. That had become my life, and I was happy with it.

On January 28, 1986, I flew as co-captain with my buddy Jim Finley on Flight 201 to Teterboro.

After diving into Chicago's Midway Airport for gas, we charged on into Teterboro to complete the mission for the night.

When the offloading frenzy was done, we left the airplane parked where it was, grabbed our bags, and locked the door. It was about nine in the morning as we climbed into our luxurious Mercury Bobcat crew car and headed a couple of blocks away to the historic Bendix Diner for breakfast – or, in our case, dinner before going to bed.

The diner had quite a reputation. It was built in 1947, and many movies, television shows, and commercials had been filmed there. One of the movies was called *Diner*, of all things. It's still there today.

The Bendix Diner, State Route 17 in New Jersey.

After breakfast/dinner (time zones can get so confusing), we drove to a hotel in Englewood, New Jersey. Off to our right, the New York City skyline and the Twin Towers of the World Trade Center stood proudly.

This particular morning the Burbank-Chicago-Pittsburgh-Newark-Teterboro crew was at the condo, so we were put up in a real hotel. No problem there, as we didn't have to change the sheets this time.

Getting to the hotel at about ten-thirty in the morning, we hit the sack. Despite it being in the middle of the day, we tried to get enough sleep so we could function that night.

It was now the 29th and I hadn't been asleep long when the telephone next to the bed jarred me out of a very nice dream.

Reluctantly putting it to my ear, I said, "What?"

Jim asked, "Are you watching the news?"

In my groggy, half-awake voice I said, "Hell no, I'm sleeping. Why?"

"It blew up. The whole thing, it just exploded!"

"What? What exploded? What are you talking about?"

"The Space Shuttle, the Challenger. It exploded after liftoff."

"Oh no. Did anyone make it out?"

"They think everybody's dead."

The loss stunned me. All those super highly qualified people – astronauts who were celebrities in our society, the best of the best. Seven lives gone, just like that, all with families and friends. Then there were the billions of dollars of equipment, a spaceship – *all lost*! Aviation took its toll again, as it always had. However, we had a job to do the next night and we had to be alert. I said, "I'll see you this afternoon."

I hung up but didn't turn on the television. Instead, I tried to go back to sleep with ugly visions of exploding space shuttles in my head.

That evening, after throwing our bags into the Bobcat, we were off to our favorite Italian restaurant. All we could talk about was the shuttle disaster. It didn't make us feel much better as we planned to jump in a high-performance airplane and streak across the night sky. Life can seem so tenuous sometimes.

In every layover town, we always seemed to eat at the same places. That was okay with me because they were always the best. Pilots, like truck drivers, always know where to eat.

After dinner, it was just a fifteen-minute drive to Teterboro Airport to preflight the airplane for the night's work.

When the trucks arrived with the checks and small package freight, we'd trade off duties. One would preflight the airplane while the other stacked cargo into the back of the cabin. Then we'd blast off, heading south. Two hours later, after landing at Atlanta, Georgia, we'd offload and take on more cargo. Then it was off to Dallas: Love Field. The routine was the same there: take on more gas, then in the air again for two and a half hours to Phoenix. If you were lucky, you had one more leg to Burbank. You'd get in at six in the morning and be done for the night, with one or two days off.

When you got into Burbank as the sun was just peeking over the eastern horizon, instead of getting to go home, you might be assigned to take the same airplane on the rest of its regular route. Either someone had called in sick or they were just short on pilots.

We took on more gas, loaded more cargo, and took off for San Francisco, where we did a quick turn-around before going back to Burbank again. Ten hours of flight time for the night and I wasn't even sure what the on-duty time was — at least twelve to fourteen hours, not including from the time you got up.

The FAA would never allow flying that many hours today, but back then, like with Imperial Airlines, operating under FAR Part 135, they got away with working us like that.

It had been a long night: six legs, down the East Coast, across the country, up the West Coast, and back down again. I was frequently impressed with the reliability of the Lear 35. It just seemed to go and go as long as you put gas in it.

On my two-hour drive home, I had a tougher-than-normal time staying awake on the crowded LA freeways. That was the most dangerous part of my job.

***

Sometimes Devarian had Learjets, Falcon 10s and 20s, and King Airs going in multiple directions at once. One of my favorite runs was the morning trip up the West Coast in the Learjet. Picking up Flight 214 from Phoenix, which was the last leg from the Teterboro run, we'd gas it up, load more cargo from banks across the country, and blast off northbound.

We were on the ground at San Francisco for only a few minutes. Then we were off to Portland, Oregon. Now lower on fuel and with very little cargo, we launched northbound out of Portland like the space shuttle. It felt like we were going straight up. One cool sensation was punching through a cloud layer, which made you feel as if you were on an express elevator to the sky, watching the clouds drop away like gravity meant nothing.

The vertical speed indicator would be pegged at six thousand feet per minute: as high as the gauge would go. From brake release to level off at twenty thousand feet took only four minutes.

As captain, I tried to make sure I flew that leg because it was such an exciting feeling to climb like a rocket. At times like this, the Lear felt more like a fighter jet, which it was originally designed as.

In the clear air, we flew over Mount Saint Helens, looking down on what was left of the blown-away portion, which still leaked smoke or steam. We always kept our fingers crossed that it wouldn't erupt again as we flew over it.

The trip to Boeing Field in Seattle took only thirty-six minutes. After getting more gas and a cup of coffee, we were back in the air. We had no cargo this time as we returned to San Francisco to spend the day.

***

Back on the other side of the country…

Cruising along through Hackensack with the windows down despite the rain and the heater going full blast, we were feeling sick. The breakfast from the Bendix Diner seemed to want to come back up. The foul odor was overwhelming, and we debated if we should just crash the car into a telephone pole, leave it there, and call a cab. However, we didn't know the address of the condo. How would we tell the driver where to go?

We'd been getting reports from other crews that the Bobcat in New Jersey was developing a nasty odor, and no one could figure out why. My suggestion was maybe the car itself had died and was decomposing.

Being in the northeast, we assumed one of those New York cat-sized rats had gotten in there and died. Having an appetite at the Bendix Diner was difficult.

After another unbearable drive to the airport, with the smell spoiling an excellent Italian dinner, I'd had enough. Before rushing into the FBO to get our plane ready, I decided to take a moment to search the car for the offending odor.

The last place I looked (it's always the last place you look) was under one of the back seats. There, I found a steak from Flower Aviation that was full of maggots. Who knows how long it had been there? At some point, the decomposition had probably expanded the plastic bag until it popped. Then the odor and the maggots started.

Disposing of the offending demonic odor did little to help the aroma of the poor car. The smell had permeated every nook and cranny. We parked it with the windows down and left the key in the ignition, hoping someone would steal it. That would have been a blessing. However, even in New Jersey, no thieves were dumb enough to steal that car.

Much to our dismay, every time we landed at Teterboro, like some kind of punishment, the stinky Bobcat was there waiting for us.

***

The poor Bobcats took a beating. They worked their little hearts out for us and rarely got any maintenance. I'm afraid we were often mean to them.

After one layover in Salt Lake City, my copilot and I lingered a little too long at dinner and realized we might be late if we didn't hustle.

I was driving that evening as we raced to the airport, and I'd forgotten about a particularly bad railroad crossing.

It suddenly loomed up on the dark street and I hit it way too fast. We became airborne like the Dukes of Hazzard.

The worn-out suspension did little to cushion our return to earth, and I saw sparks flash from underneath the car. It sounded like we'd landed right on the oil pan. It was the worst landing I'd made all week. *Good thing we were wearing seatbelts!*

Arriving at the airport, I parked the vehicle in its usual place. After we grabbed our bags out of the back seat and walked to the FBO, I looked down as I passed the front of the car. A large amount of oil was spreading across the pavement.

While my copilot preflighted the Lear, I used the pay phone in the lobby to call the office in Burbank.

The dispatcher answered. I said, "Tell the next crew to Salt Lake City that the crew car needs to be looked at. It seems to be leaking a little oil."

The almost indestructible Mercury Bobcat.

Success is where preparation meets opportunity.

~Zig Ziglar

Chapter 33
What have you got to lose?

Peering into the dark, moonless night, I saw the stars and the Milky Way shining brightly above. Far below, the lights of cities and towns glowed softly through the thin low clouds, like children reading under a blanket with a flashlight.

The Learjet's engines hummed confidently and echoed throughout the passenger compartment, which was mostly empty except for half a dozen bags of canceled checks.

It was January 1986, and I was paired again with Jim Finley. We were on one of those long, boring Burbank to Teterboro Flight 201 non-stops.

As we chatted to pass the time, Jim said, "So who are you interviewing with?"

"Oh, I'm taking my time, looking around," I lied.

He cocked his head and looked at me sideways, like he knew I was putting him off. I was.

"Everyone is hiring, you know. What are you waiting for?"

Devarian was losing pilots. Many had left to go to work for real airlines: United, Delta, Northwest, American, even Continental, Western, and Eastern Airlines.

The job market had finally opened up because of "deregulation" and the exploding Reagan economy. There was a huge demand.

Qualified pilots had a smorgasbord of airlines to choose from. Everything had changed from just a few years ago.

Trying to change the subject away from me, I asked, "Who do *you* want to work for?"

"Well, being as I'm from the East Coast, my ideal airline would be USAir."

"That's cool. Have you had an interview with them?"

"Not yet. Right now I'm interviewing with American. Man, it takes months. I've already been to Dallas for my first. There are at least three interviews with some of the toughest flight physicals in the business."

"Good luck with that. I hope you make it."

He kept pressing. "So, who are you interviewing with?"

"Well… I'm not. I'm happy where I am. I've always wanted to fly Learjets."

"Flying canceled checks when the airlines are hiring? And make a tenth as much money? Are you crazy? Besides, this place is going to go bankrupt. They're losing contracts, getting underbid by other outfits."

I looked away and stared out the windshield into the blackness of the Midwest farmland, with only a few scattered lights to reveal that any humans were down there.

I decided to come clean. "Nobody is going to hire me."

"What do you mean? You don't know that!"

"Sure, I do."

"No, you don't. What the hell are you talking about? You're a Learjet captain with thousands of hours of jet and turbine time, and you have an ATP. Why wouldn't they hire you?"

Taking a deep breath, I confessed my sins, telling him about my questionable background.

"Look, I'm a high school dropout without one day of college. I've had an altitude violation and I have a long arrest record from when I was a biker."

"Arrested for what?"

"A bunch of stuff, including attempted murder."

"Who'd you try to kill?"

"It was self-defense in a fight and not a felony conviction, but still, that was the initial charge. There's no way any airline will touch me."

"That does sound pretty serious."

"Yeah. There's a lot more on my record too, for carrying a gun and things like that. See what I mean?"

"Well, you still don't *know* that. You're just assuming."

"I do know it. There's no way."

"You should at least try."

I shook my head, not wanting to go through the heartbreak of being turned down. My default position wasn't to try even after all my success so far. I felt I'd gone as far as I could, and I was okay with that.

I said, "No, I don't want to. I'm happy here."

Jim said, "Bull! What have you got to lose?"

He just didn't understand. I said, "Okay, I'll prove it to you. I'll apply and we'll see what happens."

"Good. You'd better!"

"Who are you applying with again?"

"American."

"Okay, I'll start there."

***

On my next day off, I updated my resume and mailed it off to them, not expecting to hear anything back. Three weeks later I received an application in the mail from American Airlines.

I carefully filled it out with mixed feelings of hope and fear – hoping they might actually accept me and fearing being disappointed if they didn't. I put down all the necessary information including flight time and what kind of aircraft I'd flown.

When they asked about education, I put down, "High School Equivalent," as I'd gotten a GED a couple of years ago in Santa Rosa between fire seasons.

When they asked if I'd been convicted of a felony, I honestly answered "no." Fortunately, they asked no more about my criminal past.

My sole purpose in this exercise was to prove Jim wrong, that I wouldn't get hired. I forced myself to think the whole thing was academic.

After that, I focused on my job at Devarian, flying jets. I was happy to be there despite the sometimes-rigorous schedules, and I forgot about the application. I couldn't believe it when, a month later, I got a letter inviting me to come to the American Airlines headquarters at Dallas Fort Worth Airport for an interview.

I scheduled it for my days off. They had a seat for me on a flight to DFW and a hotel room reserved at the airport. I ran out and bought the cheapest grey suit I could afford from Sears.

My first ride on American Airlines.

Arriving at the flight academy, I sat in a big room with other applicants. I discovered the "standard" was a blue suit and a red tie. I stood out like a sore thumb in my grey suit and matching tie. I didn't know the drill.

For three days I ran the gauntlet of flight physicals, numerous interviews, and psychological tests full of bizarre questions. I later found out you could buy the answers, but somehow, I passed anyway.

There was also a check ride in a Boeing 707 simulator, the same one John Travolta trained in. It was the only working 707 sim in the country and, at the time, he owned one.

In 1986 it was an antique affair that used a closed-circuit camera "flying" over a miniature map of Chicago to provide a visual display of the cockpit windows. It had probably been around since the 1950s. They warned us, "If you crash, the camera will dig into the map board and the simulator will be down for days."

What they didn't need to tell us was, "If you crash the simulator, you'll be gone… immediately!" Game over as far as working for this airline.

At no point did they run me off, and I was finally sent home with, "Thanks, we'll let you know."

I knew it was all over, but a month after my first visit to DFW, I received another letter. It was torture opening it, as I was afraid of what it might say. To my surprise, they were asking me to come back for a second interview. The date was still a month away. Meanwhile, I went back to work, zooming around the country in the middle of the night in the hotrod Learjet.

Despite my insistence to Jim that I wouldn't get hired (or should I call it denial?), I was starting to believe I might have a chance. Wandering around the big flight academy, I couldn't help but be impressed, and I wanted to be part of it.

Two months after my first visit, I was back. The second time was much like the first, with more interviews, simulator testing, and physicals. Because of health insurance costs, they practically refused to hire smokers, and they wouldn't take your word for it if you said you didn't smoke or had never smoked. They had machines to test your lung capacity. Fortunately, I'd never smoked, though my siblings did.

Except for people like me who answered "No," the questioning went something like this.

"Do you smoke?"

"No."

"Did you ever smoke?"

"Yes."

"When did you quit?"

"Six months ago."

It was funny to listen to because the answers were always the same. They probably never got hired.

One applicant, a former Air Force fighter pilot, said he'd taken the NASA flight physical for astronauts and it wasn't nearly as tough as the physical for American Airlines.

Once again, I was sent home with no hint as to how I'd done.

I spent almost the whole year of 1986 either waiting for that "Thanks, but no thanks," or a letter saying, "Would you like to come to work for us?"

After a month another letter arrived, inviting me to a third interview. I was starting to get my hopes up.

More physicals and simulator rides ensued, but this interview also included a dreaded "Captains' Board," which consisted of three old, retired American captains with sour faces, looking down their noses at you.

They'd probably started with the company back when it was flying DC-3s, and they seemed offended that you even thought you had any kind of right to work for *their* airline.

They sat behind a long table while you stood at attention and answered their rapid-fire questions. Frequently, they criticized your answers and made you feel like you were wasting their time.

The B-scale was a two-tier pay rate in which new hires got paid a lot less than pilots already on the property. It was a sore spot for new pilots. Everyone said they didn't mind it even though they did.

When asked about it, I answered honestly. "If it wasn't for the B-scale, I wouldn't be here." And because of my background, I meant it.

Then the question I dreaded and hoped they wouldn't ask: "Have you ever had a violation with the FAA?"

I told them the truth, thinking they might already know. They acted disgusted, like I must be the worst pilot in the world.

I'm glad they didn't ask me about arrests.

Perhaps this little test was just an act to see how you handled pressure. It was working because I was sweating when I left.

That was one of the last things you had to go through before you were noncommittally dismissed again. I got the feeling those guys had the final say from the company as to whether you were worthy. I felt like I hadn't passed.

~

The captains I'd been flying with who were qualified on all three jets were making about forty thousand dollars per year. As a Lear-only captain, I was making twenty-five thousand dollars per year. I looked forward to the new type ratings and the accompanying pay increase.

It's not that it was hard to fly three different jets. The difficult part was remembering all kinds of numbers, systems, and emergency procedures if something went wrong. Confusing the wrong airplane at the wrong time could be a disaster.

There were a lot of numbers and flight characteristics to keep in your head. The big airlines allow you to fly only one type of airplane at a time.

Most of the captains at Devarian were qualified on multiple aircraft and frequently flew two or three different ones in a single night. I don't know how they did it, but somehow, they all did, seemingly with ease. I did that too but only as copilot in the Falcons.

In September 1986 Devarian offered me type ratings on the Falcon 10 and 20. With that, I would also work as captain on both those airplanes.

Two *free* type ratings were a big deal. I related earlier how they could each cost ten thousand dollars or more if you paid for it yourself. And this was back in the 1980s.

The conversation went something like this.

"Pick up the manuals for the Falcon 10 and 20 from the chief pilot's office. Your check ride will be next week."

I enthusiastically asked, "How much more will I make with the new type ratings?"

"Zero."

"No thanks."

"What do you mean? You don't want the type ratings?"

"Sure I do, but I'd like to get paid for it like the other guys."

"We can't do that. There's a pay freeze."

"I know, after the pay *cut* we've already had.

"Sorry, times are tight."

I reluctantly said, "Thanks, but I'll have to pass."

They wanted me to work harder and take more risk and responsibility while receiving no additional compensation. However, on the other hand, those type ratings were worth about ten grand a piece, so, in that respect it was kind of a dumb move.

Devarian Airways/Bancjet was having a tough time of it. There was a lot of competition from other outfits getting into the same business. They had been losing contracts to competitors.

Walking out of the big hangar, I crossed my fingers, thinking about the letter from American that hadn't come yet. Maybe there was a chance after all. I couldn't wait to get home and check the mail.

The American Airlines flight academy.

To Be Continued...

Excerpt from
Better Lucky Than Good,
Book Three

The dark cockpit lit up with a bright red light with the word "FIRE" emblazoned on it. It was accompanied by a loud bell ringing. Immediately the captain called out, "Engine fire checklist!"

The three of us bolted upright. My flight engineer seat, just behind the two pilots, was still facing forward. Having just taken off from Dallas Fort Worth Airport in our Boeing 727, we were already in the clouds at only five hundred feet in the air. We were in "instrument conditions," unable to see outside, flying only by the flight instruments and radio navigation.

Over the din of the bell, the first officer yelled, "Check essential power!" The big airliner yawed back and forth as Ron fought to keep control of it. The asymmetric thrust of the remaining engines tried to roll the airplane onto its back.

Captain Ron started cranking in rudder trim to keep the airplane straight as Bob reached up and twisted the essential power switch. Glancing up, Ron calmly said, "Essential power on Gen one, I've got the airplane and the radios. Bob, you and Dale run the checklist… and silence that damn bell."

My heart was in my throat as I grabbed the plastic emergency checklist card from its slot. I loudly announced, "Engine fire, severe damage checklist." Without waiting for a response, I started reading the items from the list.

The bell clanged on as I yelled, "Essential power selector."

Bob, the first officer, replied, "Generator One!"

Trying to focus and control my breathing, I responded with "Generators one and two online."

The engine fire was on the number three engine, the right one. I called out, "Number three thrust lever, close!"

Bob put his hand on the engine number three thrust lever and said, "Engine number three, verified?"

Ron replied, "Verified."

Yelling over the alarm bell, I called, "Number three verified."

Bob snapped the thrust lever to idle.

I called, "Number three start lever, cutoff."

Bob held the number three start lever and called out, "Number three start lever, verified?"

Ron called, "Verified!"

I said, "Number three verified," as he pulled it to the cutoff position.

Ron said, "Silence that bell, would ya?"

Bob finally hit the button on the glare shield. Without the bell, I didn't have to yell quite so loud, but the red light was still shining bright,

I said, "Engine number three fire handle pull!"

Bob pulled the fire handle back as far as it would go as Ron said, "Damnit, Bob, you need to verify that before pulling it."

Bob said, "Sorry, boss, I'm just anxious to get that fire out."

Still reading the checklist, I called, "Engine number three bottle discharge switch, push."

With his finger over the engine number three button, Bob said, "Engine number three, bottle discharge switch, verified?"

Ron said, "Verified."

I called, "Verified," and Bob pushed the number three button to shoot the fire suppression squib into the engine to try to put out the fire. The light remained on.

Ron grabbed the hand microphone and said, "Tower, American one-twenty-three, declaring an emergency. We have an engine fire, request return to DFW immediately."

Over the radio I heard, "Roger, American one two three, climb and maintain three thousand and turn left to two seven zero, report fuel and souls on board. Do you want the emergency equipment?"

I heard Ron tell him yes. Then he read off the numbers the tower had requested.

Turning us to the west started the rectangular pattern to take us back to land on runway 36L, the one we'd just taken off from.

I tried not to think about the one hundred and eighteen passengers in the back, along with the three flight attendants, and braced myself as the captain rolled the Boeing 727 hard left. I vaguely heard him calling the flight attendants, telling them we were returning to DFW and to prepare for an emergency landing.

When Bob pushed the button for the fire bottle, I hit my clock timer. Ron's conversation with the tower receded into the background as I read, "Bottle discharge light on?"

Bob responded, "It's on."

Glancing at the clock, I told Bob, "That's thirty seconds. The fire light isn't out. We need to fire the other bottle."

Bob agreed, flipping the toggle switch of the "bottle transfer" to the right. He hit the number three discharge button again to shoot our final squib of Halon fire suppressant into the burning engine. The fire light remained lit. I reset my clock for another thirty seconds.

Through the confusion, I yelled, "Captain, we're too heavy to land. Do you want me to start dumping fuel?"

Ron said, "Not until that damn fire is out. We don't want to turn into a Roman candle!"

My mouth was as dry as British humor and I wished for a drink of water, but there was no time, and we had none in the cockpit. Instead, I tried to focus on the checklist…

I hated this. I was a pilot! I'd been flying Learjets for two years before this job, and I'd flown many pilot jobs as first seat before that. I should be up front flying this airplane or at least in the copilot's seat.

Here we were, in an emergency situation, and I was sitting back at a panel, flipping switches and reading a checklist. It wasn't where I wanted to be.

I quickly pushed that out of my mind and tried to focus on the job at hand. To keep the other pilots informed and to get it on the cockpit voice recorder, I loudly read off the items pertaining to my FE panel as they were completed: "Galley switch, off, cargo heat outflow switch closed, number three pack switch off, number three generator field tripped, number three engine bleed closed."

I glanced nervously at the gauges on my panel to check the fuel balance just as Bob announced, "Fire light is out!"

Captain Ron looked back at me and said, "Dump!"

I hesitantly said, "Don't we need to let air traffic control know?"

Ron looked at Bob and said, "Tell ATC we're dumping fuel." Then, to me, he said, "Start dumping, now!"

"Yes sir, stand by. How much do you want to go down to?"

Ron said, "To the standpipes. Hurry it up, we'll be turning a base leg soon."

"Yes, sir!" I rotated my seat ninety degrees right to face the engineer's panel. Reaching to the rear bulkhead, I flipped open the small door that contained those taboo switches – the ones that poured your fuel overboard. However, there's an old saying: "The only time you can have too much fuel on an airplane is when you're on fire!'

I thought, 'Well, here we are.'

Then I remembered the special "fuel dump" checklist and madly turned the pages of the quick reference handbook until I found it.

I heard the tower say, "American one-twenty-three, turn left to one-eight-zero."

Gently banking the airplane, the captain said, "Dale, I need the "One engine inoperative landing checklist."

"Stand by." Then I announced, "Fuel dump checklist."

I felt sweat bust out in my armpits, and my collar suddenly felt very tight.

"Main tank number two boost pump switches all on! Main tanks number one and three boost pump switches both on! Crossfeed selectors number two open, number one and three closed."

I struggled to breathe and enunciate clearly because my mouth was so dry. I flipped switches and opened valves as quickly as I read the checklist.

"Fuel dump switches, all open! Fuel dump nozzle valve switches, open! Fuel quantity, monitor!"

The tower said, "American one-twenty-three, turn left zero-niner-zero."

The captain rolled the wings level on the base leg just as I reached for the "One engine inoperative checklist." Bob called out, "Engine number two is winding down. It must have ingested debris from number three!"

We were now flying on just one engine. Ron said, "Shit! Secure that engine and get me the "Two engine inoperative landing checklist. We're about to turn final!"

The airplane slewed in the air again as Ron fought to control it. We were still in the clouds, and his only references were the flight instruments in front of him. He shoved in more left rudder and dialed more rudder trim while simultaneously adding power on the number one engine.

Once again, I wondered what I'd gotten myself into and if we'd make it out of this. Pushing those thoughts from my mind, I vaguely heard the tower tell us that the emergency equipment, the firetrucks and ambulances, were ready and waiting for us.

***

Check out *Better Lucky Than Good, Book Three* to find out if we survived.

My deepest appreciation to everyone who takes the time to leave a written review on Amazon, Barnes & Noble, or Goodreads.

You can contact the author at his website.

dalearenson.com

Email, dale@dalearenson.com

Or on Facebook

Jim Aiken's Story

This didn't quite fit into the aerial firefighting chapters, but I wanted to tell Jim's story anyway, so here it is.

God's not on my side!

One day, we were sitting at the old Formica-covered metal table on the linoleum floor of the ready room inside the Quonset hut. Tanker 77 pilot Jim Eakin and I were having lunch: soup for him and a peanut butter and jelly sandwich on Wonder Bread for me. It seemed as though he always had soup for lunch.

Jim had spent a lot of time in Southeast Asia and spoke fluent Thai and some Vietnamese. It was fun to go to Thai restaurants with him, as he'd order in their language and, often, the waitresses couldn't speak it.

I'd heard he'd flown in Vietnam and, having always been fascinated with that war, I was anxious to hear more about it.

I asked, "So, you flew in Vietnam?"

"No, I was mostly in Thailand and Laos, sometimes Cambodia."

"Were you in the Air Force?"

"No, I worked for Air America."

"The CIA? You were a spook?"

"Hell no, I was just a bush pilot working for some, uh… obscure Agency for International Development. Flying supplies into remote outposts. They shut down Air America five years ago, but I'm still not supposed to talk about most of what went on."

I was disappointed. "So, you can't tell me any good stories?"

"Well, there was one funny thing I can tell you. It's not classified."

"I'm all ears."

"Okay. I usually flew the Helio Courier or the Pilatus Porter. Single-engine, short-field taildraggers that could get into and out of incredibly small runways, if you could even call 'em that. I preferred being on my own, doing single-pilot operations where I was in charge of only myself and the airplane."

I said, "Kinda like tanker flying."

"Yeah, kinda like that. But one day at the super-secret airbase in Nakhon Phanom, Thailand, my plane was down for maintenance. The dispatcher tapped me to fly as copilot for a daily resupply they called the Milk Run."

I said, "Sounds easy enough."

"Yeah, an easy day. These were flown in an old C-47, you know, the DC-3. It was based out of Vientiane, Laos. We'd be going out to some remote camps delivering cargo for the day, things like rice and ammunition. The runways weren't as small as the ones I normally went into, and that made them a little safer. The normal copilot was sick and they needed someone to fill in. They didn't care who, just needed a warm body in the seat."

Jim related that he'd already been sweating from the humidity, as the heat of the day was typically oppressive. He reluctantly showed up and met the old captain, whose name was Walt. He wasn't the talkative type. His eyes were unreadable behind his aviator sunglasses. With grey hair and a leathery, tanned face, he had probably flown DC-3s when they were brand new for the airlines in the 1930s. Or perhaps during the American Civil War.

Jim appreciated that Walt did the preflight inspection and exterior walkaround, as Jim had limited experience with the C-47 and wasn't type-rated in the airplane. He'd flown it a few times from the right seat, but the clandestine CIA airline didn't worry much about qualifications, currency, and checkouts. To them, if you were a pilot, that was all that mattered.

After climbing the ladder into the back door and walking up the steeply slanted floor to the cockpit, Jim settled into the right seat. The ground crews continued loading cargo onto the ship. The side windows were already open, but there was no breeze.

He continued: "The cockpit felt like a sauna, even early in the morning. The heat was oppressive under the sun glaring through the plexiglass, and I wanted to get going as soon as possible. I killed time by looking around at the switches and dials to familiarize myself because I hadn't flown a C-47 in a while. I found the checklist and started going over procedures that needed to be completed before we got going."

Soon Walt squeezed into the cockpit and eased into the left seat. He didn't bother to chat or get acquainted with his stand-in copilot, who, to him, was nothing more than an accessory, a required piece of equipment. Walt's eyes and hands flitted around the instruments and switches in a before-starting procedure, as if he'd done it a million times before. And he probably had.

The ground crew chief and loadmaster came up to the cockpit and had Walt sign the manifest. He said, "You're all set to go, Captain."

Walt scribbled on the clipboard and said, "Thank you, gentleman. God bless you."

Jim didn't think anything of it. He buckled his seatbelt, put on his headset, and opened the checklist to the before-starting-engine check.

However, Walt ignored him and looked out the open window at the ground crewman standing at the ready. He gave him a thumbs up.

Using hand signals, the guy on the ground indicated that the cargo door was closed.

Holding his hands up to the window, Walt closed his fists and rolled them forward – sign language that said, "Brakes parked."

Then the ground crewman pointed to the right engine with one hand. His other hand, finger pointing upward, spun in a circle: "Cleared to start the number two engine."

Jim said, "Ready with the before-starting-engines checklist, Walt."

Still ignoring him, Walt reached up to the overhead panel and expertly put his fingers on both the booster coil switch and the engine start switch. He started turning the right engine.

After it turned over a few revolutions, Walt fed the fuel to the engine. It coughed a couple of times and then fired up, belching a cloud of light blue smoke. When the smoke cleared, the ground crewman gave a thumbs up, meaning there was no fire, then pointed to the left engine with the same hand signals. Walt began turning the number one engine. It roared to life and then stabilized to a normal idle.

'This guy is a real one-man show,' Jim thought. 'No wonder the regular copilot is calling in sick.'

The ground crewman held up both hands and pointed both thumbs outward to indicate the chocks had been pulled.

Giving the guy on the ground a thumbs up, and without looking to his right, Walt said, "Tell the tower we're ready to taxi."

Jim picked up the hand mic and said, "NKP Tower, we're ready to taxi."

Nakhon Phanom Tower said, "Roger, taxi to runway One-Five. Let me know when you're ready."

Jim answered, "Cleared to taxi One-Five."

The big C-47 lumbered toward the active runway, passing an assortment of helicopters and fixed-wing aircraft on the parking ramp. There were C-123s, A-1 Sky Raiders, Cessna O-2s, UH-1s, "Hueys," and the big Jolly Green Giant helos. Most of them were there to fight in or support the top-secret war in Laos. However, they were only to deliver supplies.

Jim readied the before-takeoff checklist and waited, but Walt wasn't interested. Approaching the active runway, Walt simply said, "Tell 'em we're ready."

Jim called on the radio, "Ready on One-Five."

"Cleared for takeoff on One-Five. Good luck, fellas."

With the checklist in hand, Jim was ready to read the required items to make sure the airplane was ready to fly.

However, Walt just swung the C-47 onto the runway and smoothly advanced the throttles to full takeoff power. Soon the tail came up and they were in the air. Walt called, "Gear up, flaps up."

Shaking his head to himself, Jim complied, getting the airplane cleaned up and into flight mode.

Finally, at one thousand feet above the ground, they were making a gentle left turn above the unbelievably deep green landscape and crossing the muddy Mekong River and the border into Laos. With his jaw clenched, Jim looked at Walt. Over the noise of the engines, he yelled, "What the hell was that?"

As if acknowledging, for the first time, that Jim was there, Walt said, "What was what?"

"No takeoff checklist, no runup, no mag check, no nothing. What the hell?"

Walt calmly stared back. He smiled for the first time as he said, "What the *hell*, indeed. You don't understand, Jim. This plane will never crash. God is on my side."

Even more dumbfounded than before, Jim stared back and yelled over the noise, "No, *you* don't understand. God may be on your side, but you've got a sinner over here, and if my side crashes," he raised his voice further, "SO DOES YOURS!"

Walt turned to look back out through the windshield with a placid smile on his face as he rolled out of the left-hand turn and adjusted the throttles and props for climb-power. He knew he was dealing with a non-believer. There were so many like that, cluttering up the world. The best way to deal with them was to just ignore them.

Even being in the air, Jim thought this was the hottest day he'd ever felt in Southeast Asia.

They landed at three outposts to resupply Special Forces camps full of Green Berets with Meo or Hmong tribesmen. They were super-secret bases that, of course, the enemy knew all about. The bases and the war in Laos were only kept secret from the American people.

Every takeoff and landing went the same way. Walt flew the airplane himself and, other than telling Jim to operate the gear and flaps, he never called for a checklist or any other assistance from his copilot.

Jim had to grudgingly admit to himself that Walt was probably one of the best pilots he'd ever seen. He knew that old airplane inside and out and flew it like a conductor directing an orchestra.

There's an old saying in aviation: "The only pilots who use checklists are beginners and professionals." Jim felt the lack of any checklist was unsafe and unprofessional.

As it was, there were enough risks in their environment. Adding an extra level of risk by not doing checklists was, in Jim's mind, unacceptable.

It was after dark when they landed back at Nakhon Phanom. Jim stomped into the dimly lit ramshackle wooden shed of the operations office and stuck his finger into the dispatcher's face. In a barely controlled growl, he said, "If you ever pair me with that guy again, I'll put a two-step viper in your bunk."

The guy sat there a little wide-eyed but said nothing as Jim slammed back out through the screen door into the mosquito-ridden night. He headed for the officers' club to have a nice, stiff drink. He knew Walt wouldn't be there.

He thought to himself, 'If I can find that copilot, I'm going to have a talk with him.'

We laughed over our lunch in the Quonset hut. I was delighted to have this job and be in the company of this crazy bunch of pilots as we did an important job.

Acknowledgments

Unlike my first three books, I did not do this one all on my own.

First, I would like to thank Kathy Dishington for her tireless help in the final edit. And for her love, and sharing my life.

Thanks to Tonya Bluston, an actual editor and proofreader through Fiverr. She makes my writing look better than it really is.

Thanks to Dawn Black in Turkey for her excellent interior design and formatting, making my work look like a real book.

I would also like to thank my publicist, Andreea Billig, founder of Self-Publishing Mastery for all her help with marketing and advice as a book coach and friend.

Thanks to all of my beta readers who provided advice and critiques – especially my son Chris.

Finally, thanks to all of you readers who have read this and my other books and who give me the confidence to keep writing.

Aviation Glossary

Notes on aviation Jargon.

When it comes to numbers, we don't say "runway fourteen." We say, "One Four," or "Three Two Right, Three Six Left." They're numbered as such because of their magnetic headings of one hundred and forty, three hundred and twenty, or three hundred and sixty degrees.

Aircraft call signs aren't "Air Attack Four-Forty." It's "Four-Four-Zero" or "Tanker Seven-Six."

However, there are other times when the number is just a number. A Bell 206 is just "two-oh-six," not "two-zero-six."

A Boeing 727 can be a seven-two-seven or a seven-twenty-seven. Sometimes there are set rules, and sometimes there aren't.

An acronym like VOR isn't pronounced "Vor." It's "V-O-R," although I've heard amateurs say the former. It's like GPWS, for "ground proximity warning system," being called "Gypwis." Uh… no! We say the initials: "G-P-W-S."

ADF: Automatic direction finding, which, in the cockpit, consists of a dial that simply points a needle homing to a ground-based station known as an NDB, meaning non-directional beacon. It is the oldest air navigation system still in use today. (See NDB below.)

Airspeed: There are four kinds of airspeed.

Airspeed in miles per hour.

Airspeed in knots, or nautical miles per hour.

Indicated airspeed, which is what is read on the instrument panel. It's what the airplane thinks it's doing.

True airspeed, which is the real speed corrected for the thinner air at altitude and the temperature. "Relative to the air mass through which it is flying."

Then there's ground speed, the actual speed (miles per hour, or knots) over the ground depending on such things as air density and headwinds or tailwinds.

If you're flying a small airplane with an airspeed of a hundred miles per hour with a fifty-mile-per-hour tailwind, you have a ground speed of one hundred and fifty.

If you make a U-turn into that fifty-mile-per-hour wind, now a headwind, your ground speed will be fifty miles per hour. The cars on the interstate will be passing you.

Altitude: There are two kinds of altitude. There's **MSL,** or above **mean sea level,** which needs to be corrected for pressure altitude with an altimeter setting in inches of mercury, adjusted for temperature.

Then there's **AGL,** altitude **above ground level.** That helps to keep you from hitting things.

APU: A small turbo-shaft jet engine built into airplanes to provide electrical and pneumatic power. It allows the aircraft to operate autonomously, without ground support for cooling and engine start. Otherwise, you might have to use a **GPU,** or ground power unit.

ATC: Air traffic control. This is a service that the FAA provides to direct aircraft through sections of controlled airspace and offer advisory services to aircraft in uncontrolled airspace. The primary purpose of

ATC is to prevent collisions, organize and expedite the flow of air traffic, and provide information and other support for pilots.

ATIS: Automatic terminal information service. This is a recorded message that gives pilots all the pertinent information about airport conditions. It's usually updated once per hour, but also more often as needed. When a pilot tells the air traffic controller that he or she has the recorded information, the controller knows that the pilot does not have to repeat it.

Each ATIS recording is coded alphabetically from Alpha through Zulu.

Auto-Feather: A device that automatically turns the propeller edge-on into the wind to reduce drag on a failed engine.

Barrel Roll: Rolling an aircraft in a circle as if you were going around the inside of a barrel. If done right, it keeps positive G-forces on the aircraft. Bob Hoover could do it with one hand while pouring a glass of tea with the other.

Carburetor Heat: A system to put warm air into the carburetor to eliminate or prevent ice from building up in the fuel/air mixture as it accelerates through the venturi. Ice in the carburetor can cause the engine to stop running. Pilots hate that!

Cerberus: The mythical giant hound that guards the gates of hell.

CFI: Certificated Flight Instructor. An already commercially rated pilot who has been licensed by the FAA to teach people to fly. Some people will say "certified" instead of "certificated." A long time ago, an old instructor stressed to me, "You have a certificate, you are certificated! Meat is certified!"

CFII: The pilot is qualified to teach the much more complex instrument flying.

Coffin Corner: For jets, a high-altitude envelope in which the stall speed and Mach overspeed become the same.

Collective: The device in a helicopter that controls the engine speed and pitch of the rotor blades. It does the up-and-down stuff and is operated by the pilot's left hand.

Cyclic: On helicopters, it controls the direction of flight, similar to a fixed-wing aircraft, but does it in a different way. If you're interested, you can find a long description of helicopter controls here: https://en.wikipedia.org/wiki/Helicopter_flight_controls

Deadheading: Being sent as an aircrew somewhere, either to cover a trip or to be taken home at the end of your trip because your working trip has been canceled. You're riding in the back as a passenger but still getting paid.

Density Altitude: The AOPA describes it as follows: "Density altitude is pressure altitude corrected for nonstandard temperature. As temperature and altitude increase, air density decreases. In a sense, it's the altitude at which the airplane "feels" its flying."

On a hot day, an airport that is three thousand feet above sea level will have air so thin that the density altitude might be nine thousand or ten thousand feet.

That does two things, and they are both bad. The thinner air provides less lift over the wing, and if your airplane isn't turbocharged, an engine produces less power. Many accidents have happened when an airplane got off the ground in ground effect but was unable to climb.

DME: Distance measuring equipment. Generated from VORs or an ILS localizer.

Dumping Fuel: See **Landing Weight**.

FAA: Federal Aviation Administration. The government agency that controls EVERYTHING related to airplanes and the sky over the United States. It also coordinates with the military and foreign governments.

FARs: Federal Aviation Regulations (pronounced "F-A-R," not "far"). The national law that governs airplanes and pilots. There are different sections. Part 91 governs private pilots, while Part 135 is for intermediate commercial aviation, like Devarian or Imperial. Part 135 is the airlines and big cargo carriers. There are many others.

FBO: Fixed base operator. A business that caters to pilots and their airplanes. It sells gas, works on planes, and does practically everything you might need.

Feathering Propeller: Turning the propeller edge-on into the wind to reduce drag and stop windmilling. This is very important with a non-operating engine on multi-engine aircraft. It's even more important on single-engine planes.

Ferry Flights: To reposition or deliver an airplane empty or take it to a base for maintenance.

Flare: Raising the nose of an aircraft during landing to slow it down and put the wheels in a landing attitude.

First Officer, or FO: An important-sounding name for the copilot. Probably borrowed from the Navy. He or she is the next one in charge behind the captain.

Final Descent: There's no such thing except in the minds of flight attendants who confuse initial descent with final approach.

Flight Engineer, or FE: The third crew member, also known as a second officer or SIC, second in command. They sit behind the pilots and operate the complex systems of the aircraft like pressurization and temperature, hydraulics, and fuel. He/she must know literally everything about the operation of the aircraft except flying it. They inspect the plane before and after the flight. It requires a special license and special training.

Long ago they had to be mechanics and weren't pilots. When American hired me, you had to be a pilot, but they started you out as a flight engineer.

Today, in civil aviation, they are almost extinct as dinosaurs, at least in the United States, as computers have replaced them. All modern airliners are flown by two pilots, although on long international flights, the crew might consist of three or four pilots.

Flight Director: A computerized flight instrument that is overlaid on the attitude indicator and that shows the pilot the attitude required to execute the desired flight path. They can be used with or without an autopilot system.

Flight Following: Kind of like being on an IFR flight plan where ATC is watching over you and warning of traffic, but it's strictly a VFR procedure.

FSS: Flight service station. Operated by the FAA, they provide information and services to pilots before, during, and after flights. Unlike air traffic control, they aren't responsible for giving instructions or clearances or providing traffic separation. They do, however, relay clearances from ATC for departure and approaches. They are an important source of weather briefings for pilots.

Helo: Slang for "helicopter." Pronounced "Hilo," like the city in Hawaii.

Hood: For IFR training, a plastic device not unlike the bill of a cap, only longer. It prevents the training pilot from seeing outside to aviate (stay upright) and navigate (get where you're going), so they have to rely entirely on instruments.

Glideslope: See **ILS**.

Ground Loop: Wikipedia describes it as a rapid rotation of a fixed-wing aircraft in a horizontal plane (yawing) while on the ground, which might cause the outside wing to touch the ground. In severe cases, the wing can dig in, causing the aircraft to swing violently or even cartwheel.

Icing: Atmospheric conditions that lead to moisture in the air freezing on aircraft surfaces, propellers, and jet engine inlets. On airfoil surfaces, it degrades lift and raises stall speeds. On jet engine inlets, it can break off, go through the engine, and damage or destroy it. Many aircraft accidents have been attributed to icing.

Ident: See **Transponder.**

ILS: Instrument landing system. A precision radio navigation system that allows pilots to find a runway through clouds or other reduced-visibility conditions. Because it is so precise, commercial pilots use this method constantly, even in good weather when the runway is plainly visible. The ILS provides both vertical and horizontal radio beams. The horizontal guidance is from the localizer, while the vertical guidance is from the glideslope. They are displayed as crossed needles in the cockpit that guide the aircraft to the touchdown zone of a runway. A pilot needs special training to perform this maneuver without being able to see outside. Hardest of all is doing it in a multi-engine airplane with one or more engines inoperative. Most modern jets can land themselves on autopilot.

IFR: Instrument flight rules. Flying by instruments is primary, while looking out the window is secondary. IFR flight is regulated by the FAA with a gazillion rules and regulations. Procedures and training are significantly more complex compared to VFR instruction. Pilots must demonstrate competency in conducting an entire cross-country flight and approach to landing solely by reference to instruments. Commercial airliners operate under IFR flight plans on every flight. A pilot must not only be licensed to fly IFR but also be current within the previous ninety days. The aircraft must be properly equipped for IFR flight operations and also must have been recently inspected to qualify.

IMC: Instrument meteorological conditions.

International Officer (IO): A second copilot on long international flights, fully qualified and type-rated in the aircraft. His or her job is to spell the other two pilots so they can get some rest on long flights. The IO also inspects and preflights the plane before departure. Different airlines have different designations for this position. That is what it was called at American.

Knots: See **Airspeed**.

Landing Weight: The big jets are certificated to take off at speeds higher than they are allowed to land, due to the impact of a not-so-smooth landing. Normally they burn off their weight during flight, but if they need to land right after takeoff, some jets can dump fuel overboard to get down to their maximum landing weight. If not, they have to circle to burn it off. Even at today's gas prices, it's still bad form to throw passengers overboard, so the fuel has to go.

Layover: A stopover long enough to sleep. A two-hour connection at an airport is not a layover unless you go to a hotel room. Airline crews call a delay in your schedule a "sit."

Leading Edge Devices: Also called slats, they come out from the front of the wing to increase its camber, and like the flaps increase lift, lowering the stall speed and therefore the approach speed and takeoff speed. Along with the flaps, they turn a high-speed wing into a low-speed wing.

Localizer: See **ILS**.

Mach Number: Per Wikipedia:

Mach number (M or **Ma)** (/mɑːk/; German: [max]) is a dimensionless quantity in fluid dynamics representing the ratio of flow velocity past a boundary to the local speed of sound.[1][2] It is named after the Austrian physicist and philosopher Ernst Mach.

By definition, at Mach 1, the local flow velocity u is equal to the speed of sound. At Mach 0.65, u is 65% of the speed of sound (subsonic), and, at Mach 1.35, u is 35% faster than the speed of sound (supersonic). Pilots of high-altitude <u>aerospace</u> vehicles use flight Mach number to express a vehicle›s <u>true</u> <u>airspeed</u>, but the flow field around a vehicle varies in three dimensions, with corresponding variations in local Mach number.

Mach Tuck: If you get into a Mach overspeed situation called "Mach tuck," the nose drops and it wants to go even faster. When the supersonic shock wave gets far enough back over the wing to hit the ailerons, they can go into a flutter so fast that if you tried to grab the control yoke, it would break your wrists. You won't be able to pull the nose up to slow it down unless you grab the control column below the yoke and pull slowly, trying to slow it down.

If the airplane gets too fast, it will disintegrate in the air. Learjets were known to do that, although it was mainly the older 20 series. We were flying the newer 30 series. Like I've said, they were exciting to fly.

Microburst: A vertical wind shear, usually from thunderstorm activity. Very dangerous to aviation especially on landing or takeoff. Flying through it is like trying to go through an invisible waterfall. It can drive you into the ground and has, in several accidents that have killed hundreds of people. It was figured out only in 1985 because of Doppler radar.

Windshear/microburst recovery must be taught to pilots in simulators, and they must demonstrate the ability to recover. It's not fun!

Mixture Control: A knob next to the throttle that controls the fuel/air ratio (mixture) in the carburetor. It's used at higher altitudes to reduce the amount of fuel to compensate for lower air density: Rich for more fuel ratio, lean for less. The controls are normally set at full rich for takeoff.

N1 and N2: Two of the many gauges in modern fan jets. N1 is the fan, the high bypass portion that uses no fuel and produces more thrust than the jet portion. N2 is the jet portion, the turbine that spins at a higher rate. Both are shown on the gauges in percentage of RPMs, not actual.

A modern jet engine will be spinning anywhere from ten thousand to twenty-five thousand RPMs.

NDB: Non-directional beacon, a ground station that puts out a signal that can be used for navigation or approaches by the pilot using the ADF radio in an airplane. They're simple but effective. They aren't very precise, but even today most airports still have NDB approaches for pilots to land in IFR conditions. IFR pilots must prove competency on initial check rides and requalifying check rides.

Nomex: Fire-resistant cloth. From Wikipedia: Nomex has excellent thermal, chemical, and radiation resistance for a polymer material. It can withstand temperatures of up to 370 °C.

PIC: Pilot in command, also called the captain.

Propeller: A big fan that keeps the pilot cool. Turn it off and watch him sweat.

Runway Heading: Runway 36 means three hundred and sixty degrees on the compass heading (corrected for magnetic precession). Runway 18 is one hundred and eighty degrees magnetic. Runway 09 is due east, runway 27 is due west, and so on.

Radial: As used in navigation, a VOR has three hundred and sixty radials in all directions that you can track inbound or outbound or use in crossing an intersection.

Radial Engine: A reciprocating (piston) engine in which the cylinders "radiate" outward for the central crankcase like the spokes of a wheel. Often called a "round" engine.

The S-2 tankers that used radial engines have now been converted to use turbine engines. This has increased their load capacity, and they are now faster and more reliable.

Sectional Chart: A local chart at 1:500,000 scale made for VFR pilots to navigate visually. It provides all navigation aids and topographical information to navigate visually. Checkpoints include populated areas, drainage patterns, roads, railroads, and other distinctive landmarks. Also included are airports, controlled airspace, restricted areas, and obstructions.

SIC: Second in command. A copilot. In the airlines, they are called a first officer.

Side Slip: Cross-controlling an aircraft using a rudder and ailerons in opposite directions. Can be used to steepen a descent on approach to landing. Also used in crosswind landings where you are side-slipping the aircraft into the relative wind.

Single Engine Service Ceiling: The maximum altitude a multi-engine airplane will fly at any given weight with one or more engines out. It will vary depending on actual weight and density altitude.

Slats: See **Leading Edge Devices**.

Stall: In aerodynamics, a stall refers to the airflow **over** the wing and has nothing to do with the engine. It is the wing that holds the airplane up. The engine only propels it forward to provide that lift. If the wing stalls, the airplane will fall. With enough altitude, you can point the nose down and get it flying again. With not enough altitude, you'll hit the ground. Basic physics will get you every time. Larger, faster airplanes need a lot more altitude to recover than smaller, slower airplanes do.

Souls on Board: Live people as opposed to passengers who might be traveling in a casket (which are frequently transported by air).

S-Turns: Can be used in the air or on the ground – on the ground in a nose-high airplane so you can see where you're going. In the air, a tower controller may ask you to do S-turns on final to leave more room for another airplane taking off or landing in front of you.

TCA: Terminal control area. The airspace around large airports. This is normally very busy airspace with many commercial aircraft (usually jets) coming and going. Radio contact with air traffic control is mandatory.

Thrust Reversers: A temporary diversion of the engine's thrust. The engine doesn't reverse its rotation, just the direction of the thrust output. It slows the airplane to help in stopping and to use less brakes. It can even be used to back the airplane out of a parking space. At American we called it a "power back." Many turboprops like the Bandeirante and King Air have this capability.

Tower: Airports with an air traffic control tower control operations on and around the airport, including ground operations, usually on a separate radio frequency. Contact and participation are mandatory unless prior authorization is obtained for a Nordo (No Radio) aircraft. It's also possible to get coded light signals from the tower. Knowing what they mean is part of your training.

Touch and Goes: Practice landings in which the pilot lands and then takes off on the same runway without stopping. If you stop, it is called a full-stop landing.

Traffic Pattern: Taking off into the wind is called the "upwind leg" because you're trying to take off into the wind. Patterns can be right or left-handed. If you're staying in the pattern, your first turn is the "crosswind leg." Turning parallel to the runway is the downwind leg. Another ninety-degree turn puts you on a "base leg." Another ninety-degree turn puts you on "final approach" to the runway from which you took off. Pilots practicing landing such as touch and goes do this a lot.

Transponder: From the words "transmitter/responder." In air navigation, it's an automated transceiver in an aircraft that emits a coded identifying signal in response to an interrogating received signal from air traffic control radar. They assign you a four-digit code, and when it's dialed in, you show up on their screen as that number. When they ask you to "ident," that number flashes brightly.

Trim: Remotely moving a control tab on an elevator, rudder, or aileron to reduce the amount of pressure needed from the control yoke. For small aircraft, it's just the elevator. Larger aircraft have trim tabs in all three axes (plural for "axis"). Very important for the rudder on a multi-engine airplane.

Type Ratings: For "large" aircraft with a gross takeoff weight of twelve thousand five hundred pounds or more and almost all turbo-jet powered aircraft (airliners are both), a special addition to your license is required called a type rating. You must receive training and a check ride in each "type" to become qualified to fly as PIC or pilot in command, also known as a captain.

I ended up with nine type ratings on my license, from the little Learjet to the big Boeing 777. All are jets except for the classic old DC-3.

VFR: Visual flight rules. Simpler than IFR, looking out the window is primary, while using instruments for orientation (staying right side up) and navigation (getting where you're going) is secondary. Like with my little Cessna 140, they weren't required. VFR flying is easier and more fun.

VG Registration Numbers: Most of the airplanes at Devarian used VG after the numbers because Vic's wife was named Grace. That mean Vic and Grace adorned all the airplanes they owned. Others were leased.

VHF: Very high frequency radio.

VOR: VHF omnidirectional range. This means a radial beam for every point of the compass, three hundred and sixty degrees. You can determine your exact bearing from a station, track it inbound or outbound, or identify intersections from crossing radials of other VOR stations. It is very precise compared to ADF/NDB navigation.

V-Speeds: V is for velocity.

https://en.wikipedia.org/wiki/V_speeds

If you look at the above list on Wikipedia, you will see an amazing number of V-speeds. Just about all of them represent a speed at which you should or should not do something. Some are fixed numbers that must be memorized. Others are variable depending on several factors like weight and density altitude.

VSI: Vertical speed indicator. An instrument that indicates your rate of climb or descent. This can be very important at times.

Wet Compass: Sometimes called a whisky compass because the early ones floated in alcohol. Newer ones use kerosene. They bounce around and aren't very accurate, but in a pinch, they're better than nothing.

WAC Chart: World Aeronautical Chart, pronounced "whack." Also for VFR navigation, WAC charts have half the detail of sectional charts but cover much more territory. They have a scale of 1:1,000,000, which is about one inch = 13.7 nautical miles or sixteen statute miles. Twelve WAC charts will cover the continental United States.

The gear-up landing at Santa Rosa

United States
Department of
Agriculture

Forest
Service

RO

Reply to: 6720 Aviation Safety and Training

Date: August 10, 1981

Subject: Cessna 337 Emergency Landing Procedure

To: Forest Supervisors and Zone Aviation Officers

For your information, we have enclosed a copy of a CDF accident/incident report occuring on August 4, 1981. This involved a Cessna 337 (Air Force 0-2) aircraft.

Of special note is the procedure the pilot used to land the aircraft when the gear could not be fully extended. He feathered the propellers of both engines and turned them to a horizontal position prior to touchdown. This "heads up" thinking resulted in minimal damage to the aircraft. A "well done" goes to pilot Dale Arenson and Ranger Jerry Watson.

Please ensure that Forest Aviation Officers, Air Attack Managers, and pilots receive a copy of this letter and enclosure.

LYNN R. BIDDISON, Director
Aviation and Fire Management

Enclosure

FILE COPY
SIERRA NATIONAL FOREST
AUG 13 1981

cc: Ken Otten
Cotton Mason, CDF
Dick Harrell

The "atta-boy" from the director of aviation.

TO: ALL OFFICES
FROM: SACRAMENTO AIR OPERATIONS

8300 AIR ATTACK
8320 AIR COORDINATION

ON TUESDAY, AUGUST 4, 1981, SHORTLY BEFORE 1900, AIR ATTACK 440 (N468DF) WAS
RETURNING FROM A LOCAL FIRE AND COULD NOT FULLY EXTEND THE LANDING GEAR.

PILOT DALE ARENSON AND RANGER JERRY WATSON ATTEMPTED TO LOWER THE LANDING
GEAR MANUALLY WITHOUT SUCCESS. A DECISION WAS MADE TO FLY THE AIRCRAFT
TO THE CONTRACTOR'S MAINTENANCE BASE AT SANTA ROSA.

SEVERAL ADDITIONAL ATTEMPTS TO LOWER THE LANDING GEAR WERE UNSUCCESSFUL.
THE PILOT WAS ABLE TO RETRACT THE GEAR FULLY, FEATHER BOTH ENGINES, TURN
BOTH PROPS TO HORIZONTAL AND LAND THE AIRCRAFT ON THE BELLY SKIDS. NO
AIRFRAME OR SKIN DAMAGE RESULTED.

MAINTENANCE OFFICER DAVE WARDALL INSPECTED THE AIRCRAFT TUESDAY NIGHT AND
REPORTED THE ONLY DAMAGE SUSTAINED WAS TO FOUR BELLY-MOUNTED ANTENNAS,
THE BELLY-MOUNTED STROBE LIGHT, AND THE SKID SHOES.

CAUSE OF THE FAILURE WAS TRACED TO A FRONT ENGINE GENERATOR BLAST TUBE
CLAMP WHICH BROKE LOOSE FROM ITS MOUNTING BRACKET AND CHAFED A HOLE IN
A HYDRAULIC LINE ALLOWING LOSS OF HYDRAULIC FLUID IN THE LANDING GEAR
SYSTEM.

THE AIRCRAFT WILL BE RETURNED TO SERVICE THIS AFTERNOON.

                              G. R. LETSON, CHIEF
                              BY
                              C. W. MASON, JR.
                              SENIOR AIR OPERATIONS OFFICER

'Those Wonderful Men . . . In Their Flying Machines'

By DIANE PETERSON

By 2:30 p.m., all was quiet at the Columbia air base yesterday.

In the 90 degree heat, Air Tankers 76 and 77 stood ready for the next take-off. The sticky pink liquid fertilizer that saved the Merrihew home in Sonora just a few hours earlier hung from their bellies like stalactites.

Inside the hangar the pilots — the indisputable heroes of the day — were eating a late lunch.

Two hours earlier, they had been sitting in the same room, "doing some paperwork and enjoying the air conditioning," when a high-pitched signal called them to the scene of a blaze threatening the City of Sonora.

The pilots were airborne and over their target within five minutes.

"If we had been 20 minutes away instead of five, that house might not be there," said air base manager Jerry Watson, who directed the aggressive attack from a smaller airplane overhead.

After dropping its initial 4 tons of fire retardant known as phos-chek, each air tanker refilled twice delivering a total of 24 tons of retardant.

Norm Foster, the 44-year-old pilot of air Tanker 76, said it took him only four minutes to land, reload and take-off again.

During their attack on the hillside behind Sonora Elementary school, Foster and fellow pilot Jim Eakin sometimes dove within 100 feet of the ground.

A nine-year veteran of tanker flying, Foster was raised in southern California and has spent most of his working years in the air, from crop-dusting in Texas to chauffeuring U.S. Customs agents out of San Pedro.

He made a training movie once called "The Red Shower," and talks about his current career with unabashed pride.

"There is a sense of gratification from being able to fly aircraft low and save homes," he said, "It's just like being in combat except that they're not shooting back at you."

A button on the control yoke (steering wheel) releases the cargo.

This is the first year of work as an air tanker pilot for Eakin. A native of Pennsylvania, the 47-year-old pilot has

SEE PAGE THREE

DYNAMIC TRIO — Relaxed after a prolonged lunchtime attack on the periphery of Sonora, (from left) pilots Norm Foster, Dale Arenson and Jim Eakin pose before the S-2 air tankers, parked in front of Columbia's air base.

FROM PAGE ONE

flown for 10 years for the forest service, from Redding to Denver.

Eakin is content with his Mother Lode job so far and feels honored to have one of the 50 to 60 air tanker pilot seats in the world.

But pilots regularly risk their lives while in those seats.

"I got interviewed by Channel 5 in Sacramento," said Foster, "and they asked me if I ever had any close calls. Of course we do. When you fly low-level in smoke with lots of heat and tall trees, you can't help but have close calls."

Both the air tanker pilots and the pilot of the spotter plane, Dale Arenson, are employed by Sis Q Flying service of Santa Rosa. They are on contract with the department of forestry from the middle of June to the middle of October this year.

Arenson pilots the coordinating plane, a twin-boom Cessna, that is the first to arrive at a fire and the last to leave. His passenger, Jerry Watson, is the ranger in charge of the air base who receives target instructions from the ground and relays them to the tanker pilots.

After Watson tells the pilots where to drop, the pilots have to decide how to drop.

"He leaves the flying to us," said Foster, adding that "decisions have to be made fast because the fire doesn't stop for the air tankers."

Arenson said that when he and Watson arrived above the fire yesterday, flames were already 15 feet high and surging up the ridge to the Merrihew home.

Arenson was in the air for a total of 90 minutes yesterday.

Arenson and Watson had a close call last week when the spotter plane responded to a false alarm in Twain Harte. A hydraulic line failed and the plane's landing gear could not be lowered.

They did not attempt a landing at Columbia but flew to the company's airport in Santa Rosa, where firetrucks lined the runway for a "belly landing."

Arenson, who has flown extensively in Alaska, called the successful landing a "routine gear-up landing," but his passenger disagreed.

"It wasn't my routine," said Watson.

The captain's check ride at Imperial:

My logbook says we had a V-1 cut (simulated engine failure as you're leaving the runway, wearing a plastic hood so you can't see outside), climb out single engine, intercept an airway, still single engine, VOR approach with a hydraulic failure, and RMI (radio magnetic indicator because the NAV 1 radio had "failed" by the pulling of a circuit breaker). Then a circling approach to landing and pumping the gear down due to the hydraulic failure, then a single engine landing with reverse thrust on one engine.

This was followed by another takeoff with an engine failure and an aborted takeoff. Next came climb to altitude, airwork, steep turns, and stalls.

We did a simulated emergency descent, then an NDB approach with a holding pattern and a single-engine NDB approach. Next came a missed approach on one engine, and the attitude gyro failed. This was followed by a partial panel vectored approach to landing, single engine go around, and a single engine ILS with no attitude gyro to landing and reverse thrust on one engine. I hadn't been trained for any of these maneuvers.

About the Author

Dale Arenson is an award-winning bestselling author of gripping memoirs inspired by his risky and unconventional life. A high-school dropout, he found the supportive family he always craved as a member of the famous Hangmen Motorcycle Club. After many run-ins with the law and brushes with death and animated by the desire to better himself, Arenson reinvented himself as a commercial pilot and had a successful career in aviation for 35 years.

Always up for a good challenge, later on he became a World Champion and Record Breaker Rifle Shooter. A big admirer of classics such as Plato,

Hemingway, and Marcus Aurelius, Arenson is now taking his turn at writing books that entertain, inspire, and stand the test of time.

Embark on a thrilling journey of exploration and inspiration by venturing to www.dalearenson.com! Dive into the heart-pounding, adrenaline-fueled world of *Dale's Adventures*, where every month, you'll receive a treasure trove of exhilarating experiences, and boundless motivation. Subscribe now to supercharge your life with excitement and unshakable motivation and also get an exclusive free gift!

Also in the *From Outlaw Biker to Airline Pilot and Beyond*
Book Series by Dale Arenson

Better Lucky Than Good

Available on Amazon and all other major book retailers

Better Lucky Than Good is an inspirational story full of drama, humor, and fun flying stories. It will keep you at the edge of your seat, make you laugh and cry, and inspire you to follow your own dream.

Kindle Customer

5.0 out of 5 stars **Seat of your pants flying!**

Reviewed in the United States us on March 23, 2023

I enjoyed this author's first book, but this one blew me away! He definitely took an unorthodox path to becoming a pilot. Once again, he was able to easily describe his adventures to make this book a page turner. I cannot wait for its sequel!!

Brian Bahnsen

5.0 out of 5 stars **Thoroughly Enjoyable «Flight»**

Reviewed in the United States on January 25, 2023

Verified Purchase

I read this book with the intensity and excitement of one of Dale's many harrowing stories of a close call gone by the wayside.

The storyline captivates and keeps you engaged and interested in what is yet to come, but you sense it will be big. As an avid fan of flight, it made me feel as though I was right beside Dale waiting for instructions or guidance to escape the dilemma faced. I simply didn't want to set the book aside and enjoyed every bit of the story, and the way it was told.

An epic tale of triumph over adversity and a feel good message about doing what you dream and set your mind to accomplish.

A must read!

Dusty Beckstrand

5.0 out of 5 stars **Really exciting book!**

Reviewed in the United States on October 8, 2022

Verified Purchase

Dale had me right there with him on his flying adventures! I couldn't put it down. Edge of the seat reading.

I really can't believe that he made it through all this! I'm amazed how he went from his biker lifestyle into his exciting flying career.

He was fascinated by airplanes and wanted to fly and was up for new adventures.

He succeeded probably better than he could have imagined!

I'd like to thank him for being able to put his exciting career into writing so we can all enjoy it!

I highly recommend reading this book and his other books also.

Thanks!

5.0 out of 5 stars **Couldn›t put it down!!**

Reviewed in the United States us on December 16, 2022

Verified Purchase

What an awesome read I learned alot about small aircraft and flying well written I am following hoping for the sequel in 2023 !!

Kindle Customer

5.0 out of 5 stars **Seat of your pants flying!**

Reviewed in the United States us on March 23, 2023

I enjoyed this author's first book, but this one blew me away! He definitely took an unorthodox path to becoming a pilot. Once again he was able to easily describe his adventures to make this book a page turner. I cannot wait for it's sequel!!